Sales Forecasting
Timesaving and Profit-Making Strategies That Work

Sales Executives Club of New York

Prepared by

Harry R. White
Executive Director Emeritus

Scott, Foresman and Company   **Glenview, Illinois**
Dallas, Texas   Oakland, New Jersey   Palo Alto, California   Tucker, Georgia
London

ISBN 0-673-15948-5

Library of Congress Cataloging in Publication Data
White, Harry R.
  Sales forecasting.

  Bibliography: p. 168
  Includes index.
  1. Sales forecasting.   I. Sales Executives Club of New York.   II. Title.
HF5415.2.W46   1984   658.8'18   84-1425
ISBN 0-673-15948-5

1 2 3 4 5 6 7 – RRC – 89 88 87 86 85 84

Sales Executives Club of New York

This organization has been the recognized leader in changing the nature of selling for over fifty years, giving it a dignity and sense of professionalism that was lacking in earlier times. Long an innovator in keeping its over 2500 members abreast of the many changes impacting selling, it was also the launching pad for the marketing concept. Founded by IBM's legendary Thomas Watson, Sr., and headquartered in New York City, it is the nationally recognized center for sales, marketing, and management executives from board chairmen to regional sales managers. Its platform is one of the most sought-after in the business world.

The Sales Executives Club of New York is located at 114 East 32nd Street, Suite 1301, New York, NY 10016; the telephone number is (212) 683-9755.

Is This Book for You?

First of all, think of *Sales Forecasting: Timesaving and Profit-Making Strategies That Work* not as a book, but as a special report, a guide, a review. It was prepared on the assumption that you—the prospective reader—

> know little about sales forecasting and want to learn more about this fascinating and increasingly sophisticated marketing tool;
>
> find most of the literature on the subject rather technical and hard to digest;
>
> want to improve your present forecasting methods by adopting a few ideas from other companies and comparing their experiences and problems with your own.

If you satisfy any or all of these conditions, welcome to the majority! Research done by the Sales Executives Club of New York showed that most of its 2500 members—the elite of America's sales and marketing executives—were uninformed about all but the most elementary forecasting techniques. What's more, there was a feeling that the subject was much too technical to be of immediate concern to them. Leave it to the statisticians!

So the Club's Research Committee decided to do something about it. They asked Harry R. White, retired Executive Director of the Club, to study the experience and literature on the subject and to write a digest that is easy to understand and to put to practical use. His forty-three years of working intimately with sales executives and writing very readable reports on rather technical matters made him, in our estimation, a good choice for the assignment.

We feel he has accomplished the task we set out for him. I am one of those sales executives who thought that sales forecasting was too technical a subject to warrant my concentrated attention. And yet, as I read this report, I found myself becoming increasingly fascinated by this vital business tool, and I am impressed with the amount of information presented so lucidly and tersely in these pages.

I think you will be too.

> Edward B. Flanagan
> President
>
> Sales Executives Club of New York

Special Acknowledgment

As with any work of this nature, nothing could be accomplished without the interest and dedication of a small group of key executives—the Club's Research Committee. Under the chairmanship of Lawrence G. Chait (Director, L. G. Chait Consultants, Inc.), who guided the endless meetings, reviewed the early drafts, and kept the project moving along, go our special thanks. To Alfred Hong, Managing Director, Marketing Economics Institute, and Chuck Smith, President, Distribution by Design, our special thanks also for giving so much of their time. And to the rest of the committee members listed below—much appreciation.

Dr. Alfred Berkowitz
Department of Business
Kingsborough Community College

Ruth G. Ehrlich
Leviton Manufacturing Company

John D. Faulkner
Case & Company, Inc.

Gerald Frisch
Gerald Frisch Associates

Clark Lambert
Citibank

Abraham Landau
A. J. Landau, Inc.

Lou Moskowitz
Admar Research Company

John S. Reed
I.C.I. United States, Inc.

Thomas A. Taylor
T. A. Taylor Company

Dr. Robert F. Vizza
School of Business
Manhattan College

Contents

1

About Forecasting—
and This Report

1a Why Forecast?

"The moment you forecast, you know you're going to be wrong; you just don't know when and in what direction," quips economist Edgar R. Fiedler. "The person who lives by the crystal ball has to learn to eat ground glass."

True, anyone who forecasts will produce forecasts that are sometimes wrong, whether they are economic forecasts, weather forecasts, sales forecasts, or any other kind of forecast.

So why forecast at all if you know that the chances are you might be wrong? The answer, of course, is to *reduce risk*. As a business executive, you have to allocate resources today whose return is based on some expected outcome in the future. Forecasting reduces the risk of the decision by using every available tool to anticipate the most probable outcome.

For the businessman, reasonably accurate sales forecasting is indispensable to good management, whether the company is a one-person operation or General Motors. Besides being an asset to the company, good forecasting has a direct bearing on the nation's economic well-being. You hear many stories of overly optimistic sales forecasts resulting in heavy inventories that have not only hurt the businesses themselves but also contributed to causing "inventory recessions" that become a drag on the economy.

A recent example of this was the failure in 1979 of the American automobile industry to forecast the demand for small cars. This resulted in huge inventories of large cars, layoffs of thousands of workers, and the triggering of a mild national recession. Chrysler Corporation, with a 104-day backlog of 80,000 cars in July of 1979, was close to bankruptcy. And the Japanese and other foreign small car makers were further entrenching themselves in the American market. As this was written in 1983, the auto industry faced a new unforeseen challenge—to supply the demand for larger cars due to the abundance of gasoline and improvement in the economy.

1b   Science or Art?

Has sales forecasting advanced to the point that it can foresee such trends and be called a science?

Since computers became readily available around 1960, the accuracy of sales forecasting has increased remarkably. New techniques have proliferated like mushrooms. Economists, mathematicians, and university professors have come up with a dazzling array of them—with jargon to match—that bewilders the average sales executive. A spate of books and business magazine articles on the subject—most of them published since 1960—attempt to enlighten; but some knowledge of mathematics and statistical and economic theory is required to understand most of them.

True, sales forecasting has become much more "scientific" in the past two decades. But it is still very much an art. A system that works fine in one company may be inadequate or a dismal flop in another. And no one has yet come up with a substitute for the most important element of all in sales forecasting—good executive judgment.

As a topic of discussion, sales forecasting has been sadly neglected by sales executives and by sales executives clubs. In his 43 years with the Sales Executives Club of New York, your author can recall no meeting or seminar specifically devoted to this subject. Perhaps that's because it was felt that sales forecasting was the province of the statistician. The sales department's concern with preparing forecasts was usually limited to estimating how much they expect customers to buy in the year ahead (for more on this, see Section 3c).

With sales forecasting gaining more and more importance along with its increased complexity and accuracy, the Research Committee of the Sales Executives Club of New York felt that something should be done to make executives more aware of the state of the art and how it works. As a first step, a survey of members' sales forecasting practices was undertaken. Out of it grew this book.

1c   Objective of This Report

What we shall attempt to do here is to give you an *abbreviated view* of current sales forecasting practices and problems—some of it in checklist form. We will assume that you are the typical busy sales executive who knows little about the technical side of sales forecasting but would like a quick look at what it's all about. We'll skip some of the more highly technical refinements and give you formulas only where necessary to understand how a basic forecasting method works.

If you wish to delve further into the details, there is a list of books and business publication articles at the end of this report. We especially recommend the Conference Board's publication, *Sales Forecasting*, which is replete with case histories, charts, and formulas. Publication information is found in the Bibliography.

You'll also find in the back of this report a list of definitions of terms commonly found in sales forecasting literature. This may be helpful to you in reading other books and articles on the subject. It will also serve as a review of some of the techniques and vocabulary of this fascinating new art-science.

2

Sales Executives Surveyed

What are the various methods of sales forecasting? Which are the most frequently used in your type of business? How often are forecasts made? Who makes them? How could you make your sales forecasts more accurate? What are the most vexing problems for forecasters of existing and new products or services?

These and scores of related questions were put to the 2300 members of the Sales Executives Club of New York in a nine-page questionnaire. A total of 222 responded—about 10 percent, which is considered a good return for a questionnaire of this length and complexity. An analysis of the respondents done by Alfred Hong of the Marketing Economics Institute indicated that they were not only representative of the membership of the club but also a fair cross-section of American business as a whole.

Replies were tabulated by total response and by size of company in three categories—small, medium, and large (see the Box on page 6). We attempted a further analysis by type of business—consumer, industrial, and service. But we ran into a common bugaboo in the study of sales forecasting. Many companies look upon their forecasts and forecasting methods as trade secrets. So, while all respondents indicated their company size, many refused to identify themselves further. And sixteen indicated that they even keep their forecasts from the eyes of many of their executives, as well as their sales staffs. This secrecy is perhaps understandable when you consider that *concern about the competition* was one of the problems of forecasting mentioned most often by our respondents.

The questionnaire summaries presented in this report should be considered as *indications* of how 222 sales executives do their sales forecasting and what they see as their major problems in trying to predict their sales. They should not be considered as showing the right method or wrong method. That's because each company's method of operations and requirements are different and what's good for the majority may not necessarily be good for you. But if you suspect that your forecasting could be improved, it might be a good idea to consider what other companies in your league are doing.

2a   General Observations from Our Survey

Here are some of the general observations we have drawn from the responses to this study:

The less sophisticated methods of forecasting are used by the majority of companies, even larger ones with many product lines.

Most companies rely on more than one technique of forecasting. Their experience evidently shows that certain methods are better for individual product or market situations. Also, more than one set of calculations are found useful to improve the accuracy of a forecast.

Over one half of all companies have had a sales forecasting accuracy of 90 percent or better over the past five years. Accuracy usually increases as the company gets larger.

Most forecasts are expressed as single-point estimates, rather than in terms of ranges or probabilities.

Most sales executives are confused by the more technical types and terms of forecasting procedures, such as econometrics, exponential smoothing, time-series analysis, and the like. (In the following pages, we will try to explain these and other such methods in non-technical language.)

3

Results of Sales
Forecasting Survey

About Our Survey Figures

Figures derived from the Sales Executives Club of New York Forecasting Survey are presented in this report as *percentages* of each size group of respondents, plus percentages of all responses. This should make for easier and more accurate comparison, since there is considerable difference between the number of responses in each group. The group parameters, plus the number of responses, are as follows:

Small-Size Companies: Those with annual sales volume under $10-million. (52 responses)

Medium-Size Companies: Those with annual sales volume over $10-million but under $50-million. (64 responses)

Large-Size Companies: Those with annual sales volume over $50-million. (106 responses)

3a   What is the Usual Forecast Frequency?

	All	Small	Medium	Large
Annual forecasts	87.7%	84.6%	84.3%	94.3%
with weekly revisions	3.3	0.	6.2	3.8
with monthly revisions	24.7	19.2	17.2	37.7
with quarterly revisions	36.5	32.6	37.5	39.6
with semiannual revisions	17.3	23.	14.	15.
Two-year forecasts	10.2	13.	6.2	11.3
Five-year forecasts	25.5	13.	20.3	43.3

As you can see, the majority of companies in our study have annual sales forecasts with quarterly or monthly revisions. These figures are presented simply as a matter of interest rather than to suggest that the best forecasting frequency for your company might be the one most used. Even in the same size and type of company, the mix and diversity of forecast intervals is considerable. For instance:

- A small cosmetics manufacturer has an annual forecast with a semiannual revision and monthly reassessments.
- A large grocery manufacturer with an extensive product line forecasts four years ahead, with a forecast for each year by product line, plus a forecast for the coming year for each individual product on a month-by-month basis. Four-year forecasts are issued nine months ahead and updated four months ahead. Accuracy has been between 95 and 99 percent!
- A large service organization does a five-year forecast, revised and implemented by annual forecast and performance statistics.
- A small paper goods distributor makes informal forecasts for one, two, and five-year periods, with accuracy ranging from 75 to 89 percent.
- A small pharmaceutical goods company makes annual, two-year and five-year forecasts, with 95 to 99 percent accuracy.
- A large tobacco products company makes annual, five-year and eight-year forecasts.
- A large pharmaceutical products manufacturer makes annual forecasts with quarterly reviews, plus two-year, five-year, and ten-year projections.
- A large consumer goods company makes long-term forecasts based on

historical data and general business outlook; short-term forecasts on line review data and orders to date.

A large industrial firm uses a rolling twelve-month forecast, updated each month.

A large service company has an annual forecast with four-month rolling updates.

Taken as a whole, companies evolve the forecasting frequencies that best suit their type of product, market, and method of operation. There is no one "best" frequency mix.

In determining or reviewing your company's frequency of forecasting, here are some things to bear in mind:

If your market is a stable, slower-moving one, your forecasting span should be longer-range. In this type of market, a two-year forecast might be considered short-term, whereas in a faster-turnover market it might be considered long-term.

If you're a manufacturer, you're probably using monthly, quarterly, or semiannual forecasts. If you're a nonmanufacturer, you're probably working only with annual figures.

If you're in a business that requires major capital investments to get rolling—such as a utility—you will probably need to forecast beyond a five-year period.

If getting market information is difficult in your business, you may have to be satisfied with an annual forecast without updating.

If your business is such that you get continuous market and sales information more or less automatically, you will find quarterly or monthly forecast revisions possible without too much effort.

Thanks to the abundance of computers and computer services, most firms make some kind of short-term forecast, usually in monthly or quarterly units extending over the next few months or quarters. Since purchasing, production, and pricing are usually keyed to this forecast, it is commonly known as the *operating forecast*.

Company Example
United Steel & Wire Co.

Planning Ahead with a Five-Year Forecast

United Steel & Wire Co. of Battle Creek, Michigan, is typical of the medium-sized company that tries to determine its future equipment and man-power needs with simple forecasting methods. Every year, they study the sales figures for the past five years and then project what they might reasonably do over the next five years. The first three years of the forecast are considered the most important, because anything in the line of new equipment has to have a payout of no longer than two-and-one-half years. The last two years of the forecast are frankly "guesstimates," but they at least provide goals that the company might plan for.

Every six months, the three-year forecast is updated to reflect current conditions. The basic input data comes from the salespeople and sales managers, whose estimates have been "pretty much on the beam," according to vice-president George L. Stierle. These estimates are routinely adjusted by top management to allow for overoptimism or underoptimism observed in the past. Sales quotas are based on these estimates.

Another important element of the US&W forecast is account initial orders, where initial orders received early in the selling period are compared with initial orders received the year before from a matched sample of customers. They report that their most reliable industry figures to estimate share of market come from trade publications.

3b   How Accurate Have Your Sales Forecasts Been?

(Over a five-year period)

	All	Small	Medium	Large
100%	0.45%	.0%	.0%	0.94%
95–99%	23.2	11.5	28.1	30.1
90–94%	26.1	23.	23.4	32.
75–89%	33.6	40.3	35.9	24.5
50–74%	9.2	11.5	9.4	6.6
Less than 50%	1.8	3.8	1.6	0.

What Factors Affect Forecast Accuracy?

Formal training in forecasting is the single largest factor affecting forecast accuracy.

As the level of forecast preparation moves upward to corporate headquarters, accuracy improves.

The use of sophisticated techniques as opposed to the simpler techniques does not significantly affect forecast accuracy.

These are some of the findings of a study of 160 companies done for the National Council of Physical Distribution Management by John T. Mentzer and James E. Cox of Virginia Polytechnic Institute and State University. Results were reported at the Council's annual conference in New Orleans in October 1983.

Other factors affecting forecast accuracy revealed by the study:

 Accuracy suffers as the forecast gets down to individual product forecasts.

Accuracy is not significantly affected by the need to make, in many cases, thousands of forecasts as opposed to relatively few.

As the time horizon increases, that is from monthly to yearly or bi-yearly forecasts, accuracy decreases significantly.

 Wholesale and retail industries have higher forecast accuracy than manufacturing industries, probably because of closer contact with their markets.

Observations:

The larger the company, the higher the degree of forecasting accuracy, because of the more sophisticated methods of "tracking" of data and analysis.

Forecasts for a company as a whole are usually more accurate than those for divisions of the company or individual lines of products or services.

Much of the potential accuracy obtainable is beyond the control of the forecaster and lies in the sales data used. Are there fluctuations caused by significant seasonal and trend patterns? Is record-keeping complete and up-to-date?

Of special interest is the finding that the use of more sophisticated (that is, complex) techniques adds very little to forecasting accuracy. Caution Messrs. Mentzer and Cox: "The considerable amount of computer and forecaster time necessary for the more sophisticated techniques should lead managers to carefully evaluate their usefulness to the company." This conclusion is further supported by the results of the International Forecasters' Competition sponsored by the *Journal of Forecasting* in 1982, which showed that, on the whole, the simpler models did just as well, if not better, than the complex ones in forecasting 1,001 time series. (See *Journal of Forecasting,* Volume 1, Number 2, April–June 1982.)

The authors of the report were impressed with the finding that formal training in sales forecasting showed as the most important factor affecting forecast accuracy. They conclude: "The results should have clear implications for managers when considering the importance of forecasting courses or seminars for their forecasters. The more formal training received, the greater the forecast accuracy."

The most accurate forecasts are those for standard consumer necessities with established markets, usage patterns, or brand loyalties. Forecasters of industrial components have a particularly hard time because they have to estimate demand for items that go into products that, in turn, may be parts of other products.

Some companies consider more accurate forecasts less important than forecasting consistency. They feel they can get along all right as long as their forecasts fall within familiar margins.

If a company's markets are affected by long-term ups and downs (cycles), it may be more interested in pinpointing the turning points in market demand than in the accuracy of forecast figures.

In some companies, the sales forecast is considered a goal to be achieved, thus becoming a "self-fulfilling prophecy."

While a great many variables can affect the accuracy of your sales forecasts, two basic questions to ask are the following:

How *available* are data about your market?

How *reliable* are the data you use? (Methods of measuring the reliability of out-of-company data are outlined in Section 10 on Econometrics.)

3c Who Is (or Are) Responsible for Sales Forecasting in Your Company?

	All	Small	Medium	Large
Chairman or President	15.9%	38.4%	9.4%	0. %
V.P. or Director of Marketing	40.7	30.7	59.3	32.
V.P. of Finance or Controller	.6	0.	0.	1.9
Director of research	.6	0.	0.	1.9
Sales manager	19.1	13.4	15.6	28.3
Product manager(s)	7.4	1.9	6.2	14.1
Company economist	.6	0.	0.	1.9
Combination of executives	25.6	15.3	25.6	35.8

Based upon the above information:

In the small company, sales forecasting is usually done by the chairman or president.

In the medium-size company, the vice president or director of marketing usually has the responsibility.

In the large company, forecasting is most often done by a group of executives. This is also true, to a lesser degree, of the small and medium-size companies.

There seems to be a growing trend in all companies to get *more participation* in the forecasting process. By doing this, they not only get input from those who can make good contributions to the forecast, but also assure greater acceptance of the forecast and commitment to the plans based upon it.

3d Do You Use an Outside Consulting Service to Perform or Implement Your Sales Forecasts?

	All	Small	Medium	Large
Do entire forecast	0. %	0. %	0. %	0. %
Assist in forecast	3.9	1.9	3.1	6.6
No consultants used	92.6	92.3	96.9	88.7
No answer	3.5			

It seems obvious from this response that forecasting is one area of business activity in which outside consultants are seldom used. When they are consulted, it's to recommend better forecasting methods or to fortify the company forecasts with special expertise or an outside viewpoint. Emery Worldwide, for instance, has had a long-time relationship with a consulting firm that provides it with economic forecasts. And Bristol-Myers uses an outside service to augment its forecasting (see Company Example on page 34). Where new products are involved, the use of outside services is more frequent (see Section 11 on New Product Forescasting).

3e How Far in Advance of the Beginning of the Forecast Time Period Are Your Sales Forecasts Issued?

	All	Small	Medium	Large
1 month	18.5%	11.5%	15.6%	25.5%
2 months	20.3	21.	25.	15.
3 months	29.8	32.7	26.6	30.1
4 months	6.	1.9	7.8	8.5
5 months	3.2	1.9	3.1	4.7
6 months	13.1	13.	14.	12.3
Other	9.1	—	—	—

Distribution one to three months in advance seems to be the favored range, with a three-month lead being the most common among our respondents.

Among forecast distribution practices reported:

A large consumer fabrics company issues its forecasts anywhere from three to six months ahead, depending on market conditions.

A large consumer goods company issues its forecasts two or three months prior to the year end.

A medium-size industrial firm issues its forecasts ten months before the beginning of the forecast period.

A large confectionery manufacturer issues its forecasts one year in advance.

A large consumer goods firm issues forecasts three months ahead for production planning, and one month ahead for the sales department.

Here again the practices of the majority are no assurance of the "right" or "best" method. The right advance time for issuing your forecasts is whatever you have found works best in the past. In recent years, sales forecasting techniques have developed so rapidly that forecasters have acquired the *smorgasbord approach*—helping themselves to whatever goodies they can absorb or afford. The miracle of data processing has made the monthly and quarterly forecast update commonplace, so that in a great many firms— especially the larger ones—sales forecasting has become a *continuous process*.

The Gere Accuracy Recipe

William S. Gere Jr., the management science specialist, says it can be statistically shown that three unbiased forecasts made separately, then averaged with appropriate weights, are apt to produce accuracy with a narrower margin of error than any one forecast by itself. One of the companies that uses this method is Uniroyal, Inc., which makes three separate monthly forecasts— one by exponential smoothing of sales figures, another by using economic indicators, and the third by fitting a least-squares trend curve to quarterly sales. Each forecast is weighted in accordance with the technique's previous record of reliability and the results are averaged. (See *Sales Forecasting*, The Conference Board, pages 205–210.)

3f   Who Receives Copies of the Sales Forecast?

	All	Small	Medium	Large
All executive personnel	64.4%	53.8%	73.4%	66. %
Only the "top brass"	15.	23.	10.9	11.3
Product managers	26.1	9.6	23.4	45.3
Purchasing manager	9.7	0.	10.9	8.5
Production manager(s)	23.7	11.5	31.2	28.3
Field sales managers	33.7	15.3	31.2	54.7
All salespeople	19.3	19.2	17.1	21.7
We keep our forecasts highly confidential	7.3	13.	3.1	5.7

Reflected in these figures is the growing tendency to get more and more key people in the company involved in sales forecasting.

Only 15 percent of all companies restrict distribution of their forecasts to top brass. And 7.3 percent keep their forecasts highly confidential. These percentages are considerably greater in the small companies, where competition is more keenly felt and a copy of a competitor's sales forecast could be a tip-off of its selling or production strategies in the near future.

Rather a surprise is the low spot the *purchasing manager* takes on the totem pole. This oft-neglected partner of the management team must be kept better informed of anticipated sales potentials in order to do a really effective job of buying the goods and services needed to achieve those potentials.

3g   What is the *Real* Purpose of Your Sales Forecast?

	All	Small	Medium	Large
To derive a true assessment of the market potential	30. %	21. %	31.2%	37.7%
To serve as a goal-setting device—statement of desired performance	64.6	67.3	62.5	64.1
No answer	5.4			

This illustrates the difference of opinion that exists about the basic objective or purpose of the sales forecast. Should the approach be to assess the potential of the market, or should it serve as a statement of what management expects in the way of increased sales or profits—a built-in sales goal that becomes a "self-fulfilling prophecy"? About two-thirds of our respondents indicate the latter view of their forecasts. Some said their forecasts have both objectives.

Here is a sampling of some of the comments on this issue:

To set goals combining an assessment of the market, the sales force potential and our profit objectives. (small cosmetics manufacturer)

A realistic statement of what we hope to see accomplished in the year ahead and how we will accomplish it (marketing plan) and what tools will be needed (promotion). Also serves as a review of the year just ending and a time to discuss market changes. (large sales agency—grocery products)

We use it as a base for our profit planning. (large industrial company)

A basis for our production and inventory requirements and cash forecasts. (large consumer goods company)

To predict our production inventory and raw materials and money required to maintain it. (medium-size consumer goods firm)

To insure full capacity, proper inventory, and to maximize profit. (medium-size industrial firm)

If the forecast is not an effort to assess the true potential of the market, but rather a sales-goal-setting device, how can you tell in subsequent years whether or not you set your goals high enough? (large consumer goods company)

3h   Besides Forecasting Potential Sales Volume, To What Other Uses Are Your Sales Forecasts Put?

(Listed in order of total number of mentions)

	All	Small	Medium	Large
Budget preparation	88.8%	90.3%	87.5%	88.7%
Setting quotas for salespeople or territories	67.	61.5	67.1	72.6
Determining expansion or reduction of facilities	58.	44.2	67.1	63.2

	All	Small	Medium	Large
Determining advertising and sales promotion expenditures	50.	55.7	40.6	53.8
Hiring (or laying off) of personnel	47.9	59.6	45.3	38.7
Advance purchasing of raw materials or parts	47.7	28.8	53.1	61.3
Determining investment requirements	43.9	38.4	40.6	52.8
Setting quotas for product lines	43.7	30.7	43.8	56.6
Determining products or services to be phased out	30.4	23.	34.3	34.

Others mentioned:

To make cash forecasts. (large consumer goods firm)

To realign sales territories and determine types of new customers to be solicited. (large sales agency)

To set production schedules. (medium industrial company)

To develop our overall division operating plan. (medium industrial company)

Where's the Financial Executive?   It's no surprise that budgeting heads the list of other uses to which sales forecasting is put. How can you make up a realistic budget without knowing what the company's sales expectations and goals are? And how can you estimate your sales without knowing what amounts can be budgeted to cover the expenses of getting those sales?

But, assuming that the *financial executives* of the company are most directly involved in budgeting, why is their role in sales forecasting so minuscule (six-tenths of one percent, according to the tally in Section 3c)? Of course, the "combination of executives" figure of 25.6 percent undoubtedly includes the financial experts to some degree. But it would seem good sense to make sure that they are prominently included in all forecasting decisions, especially the final steps where sales and profit goals are set. And the primary concerns of their office—cash inflow, profits, dividends, expense control, capital outlays—all are in essence determined by sales volume.

In Trying to Get More Accurate Sales Forecasts, What Element Do You Find Gives You the Most
3i Trouble?

(Listed in order of total mentions)

	All	Small	Medium	Large
Inability of salespeople or their managers to judge their sales prospects accurately	33.2%	30.7%	40.6%	28.3%
Actions of competitors	30.8	26.9	25.	40.6
State of economy	29.5	30.7	25.	33.
Lack of reliable industry figures	16.4	21.	18.8	9.4
Influence of trends or fads	15.1	19.2	14.	12.2
Changes in government policy or government regulations	13.5	13.	7.8	19.8
Effectiveness of advertising and sales promotion	12.8	17.3	6.2	15.
Wide divergence of opinion in management	10.7	9.6	9.4	13.2
Influence of weather	8.7	7.7	10.9	7.5
Difficulty in gauging consumer preferences	8.3	11.5	7.8	5.7
Effectiveness of distributors or dealers	7.6	13.	3.1	6.6
Size of inventories of distributors or dealers	6.1	3.8	6.2	8.5
Lack of know-how in computer use	2.6	1.9	3.1	2.8

The respondents mentioned other difficulties:

Top management lag time in realizing realistic growth objectives. Persistence of "boom" mentality. (large grocery products firm)

Inability of manufacturing to produce product lines to realize sales goals. (large consumer goods firm) [Question: Is manufacturing consulted in setting these goals?—Ed.]

Communications lag. Manufacturers we represent give us insufficient lead time for new product introductions, competitive pricing changes, policy changes, supply shortages, etc. (large consumer goods sales agency)

Outcome of union negotiations with our major customers. (medium-size industrial company)

Inability to reach end-user market with factory or distributor sales forces. (medium-size industrial company)

Branded vs. unbranded goods. Unbranded easier to forecast, projecting industry totals and estimating our market share. Branded requires complicated correlation analysis, plus consumer research. (large grocery firm)

Inability to find good leading indicator. Our sales seem to run at least three months ahead of the general production index. (large chemical firm)

Each department head forecasts on basis of own assumptions. We hope to set up standards for forecasting and an audit function to cross-check estimates of department heads. (large industrial company)

Inability of salespeople to judge their prospects accurately—that problem took first or second place with most of the companies interviewed for this study. Since input from the sales department is important to the forecasting process, most companies try to adjust for over- or under-estimation with formulas based upon how individual salespeople forecasted in the past, or with the use of executive judgment. Also, some companies use incentives to reward salespeople for forecast accuracy. More on this subject will be found in Section 6.

Taking second place in the list of forecasting problems is the *actions of competitors*. Needless to say, an entire forecast can be obsoleted by a competitor's major action. Companies in highly competitive fields often find that short-term forecasts are needed to keep abreast of such moves.

As noted previously, the concern about competitive action or counter-action becomes almost obsessive in some companies, to the point that sales forecasts are considered proprietary secrets to be guarded from the eyes of competitors and, in some cases, of most company personnel.

Sales Force Estimates

What are the estimates of salesmen and their managers?

Are they modified by past experience to allow for over- or under-estimating?

Economic Indicators

Are there any economic series, such that housing starts, that lead our sales figures?

How can we correlate these to show a predictive effect?

Sales History

How much did we sell in previous periods?

Can we project past performance into the future, using moving averages?

Trend & Cycle Analysis

Can we use more sophisticated methods of time series analysis to identify and give numerical values to the "factors of change" in our sales history — long-term trends, cycles, and seasonal patterns?

Polling of Customers and Prospects

Can we get reliable estimates from distributors and other customers and prospects?

Can we estimate the trend of sales by initial orders?

What are the needs of the end-users of our products?

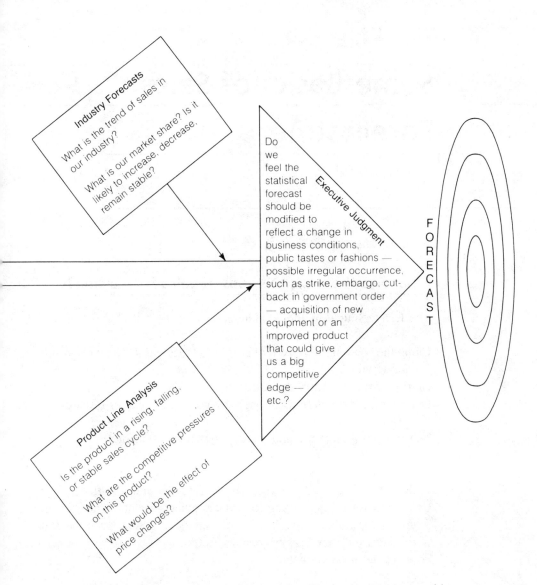

Figure 3.1. Use These Inputs to Improve Your Forecasting Marksmanship

4

Some Basics of Sales Forecasting

4a What Are the Basic Methods of Sales Forecasting?

The less technical methods include:

Using the personal judgment of a knowledgeable individual or group of individuals
Getting estimates from the sales force
Determining expectations of users by polling or market research

The more technical methods (computers usually needed):

Using time-series analysis—observing past sales figures and averaging them to get a trend line that can be extended into the future
Using econometrics—trying to find a predictive relationship between your sales and an outside series of statistics, such as Gross National Product, industry figures, housing starts, etc.
Forecasting new products

The less technical methods of forecasting are the most widely used. Many companies use more than one method; some use every one of them. The more methods you can use—or afford to use—the more accurate your forecasts will probably be.

4b   Seven Basic Policies of Successful Forecasters

What's the difference between a successful and a mediocre forecasting system? In studying the methods used by the hundreds of companies that contributed information to this book, we found that those who are most satisfied with their forecasting follow certain basic policies. Any company, large or small, can adopt these policies without having to acquire expensive computer set-ups or statistical wizards. What it amounts to is a philosophy of forecasting that seems to produce the best results. Here are the seven "basics":

1.   Stick to Familiar Formats

Determine what methods of presenting your forecasts you're going to use and stick with them. Keep the forms used as standard as possible so the people who contribute to the forecasts and those who use them will have no difficulty understanding them and relating them to previous forecasts. Companies that are always trying different methods and forms increase the difficulty of understanding and using their forecasts. One large financial firm that switched its forecasting to an econometric model made their computer-generated reports as close as possible in format to those that the executives were used to seeing, and made a special effort to eliminate all unnecessary technical verbiage.

2.   Make Your Forecasting a Team Effort

A successful forecast depends on the inputs from as many key company personnel as possible. The sales force and sales managers provide estimates direct from the field (usually discounting a certain amount for overoptimism or overpessimism). The research people give vital clues to changing patterns of consumer behavior. The marketing department tells you what you might expect in the way of market shifts and swings in the economy. The financial department advises of budget requirements and any money problems entailed in reaching forecast levels. The production department foresees any manufacturing or service bottlenecks that could knock a forecast off course. And the "feel for the market" of seasoned top company executives is probably the most important input of all.

3.   Put the Accent on Accuracy

Remember that a major function of the forecast is to determine how money and other resources shall be budgeted and how much should be produced to avoid overstocking or stock-outs. Many companies upset this objective by considering the forecast as a sales goal to be exceeded, if possible, with incentives for performing above forecast. This sometimes leads to underestimating, stock shortages, and insufficient financing. Successful forecasters reward accuracy and let everyone in the company know how important it is.

4.   Know Your Past to Know Your Future

Your basic forecasting tool is data on company sales in the past. Is the trend up, steady, or down? How have sales been influenced by seasonal factors, style changes, competitive actions, and the like? What forecasting methods have worked in the past—and what didn't? What forecasts were wide of the mark and why? Knowledge of the past improves knowledge of the future.

5.   Anticipate Change

If there's anything you can count on in these fast-moving times, it's change. So successful marketing programs and action plans anticipate change. Is there a shift in the market toward different products or innovations? How will competition affect your sales? What will be the effect of new advertising and sales promotion strategies on sales volume? If your business or industry is subject to radical change, it might be more advantageous to have your forecasts expressed in terms of ranges or possibilities rather than single-point estimates.

6.   Experiment

While a good forecasting system discourages constant tinkering based on whim, it also encourages the open-minded consideration and testing of other methods or inputs that might improve forecasting accuracy. These might be such things as an economic indicator with better predictive powers than one you're now using, "backcasting" to determine why errors were made in past forecasts, or experimenting with formulas to adjust your estimations to seasonal factors, economic swings, or any special hazards of your line of business.

7.   Keep Up To Date

Good forecasting systems provide for constant tracking, updating, and self-correction, particularly in businesses with broad-based and volatile markets. If annual or six-month forecasts get wide of the mark, consider quarterly, monthly, or even weekly updates. Constantly check your input data to be sure it is current and reliable. If unforeseen changes occur in your business or markets, don't hesitate to issue interim reports revising your original estimates.

4c   Sales Forecasting Methods

To summarize, what questions should you ask about your sales forecasting methods?

Are my *facts and figures reliable* by past experience and protected from misuse?

How Consistent Are Your Sales Results?

When using your company sales history as a base for sales forecasts, it's a good idea to check on the internal consistency of actual sales results. According to Charles W. Smith, a distribution systems counselor, once any basis for classifying geographic markets by type and size has been developed, the ratio of actual sales to base data provides a solid foundation for later estimates on where to look for increased sales. Many companies can improve their sales forecasts simply by improving their methods of defining market areas and tracking shipments. This is true particularly of companies that use wholesale channels and don't really know where their products are being used, or sold at retail.

Am I using *all the data available* from outside sources, such as a trade association, trade publications, Department of Commerce, etc., to determine more accurately my sales potential and the various factors that will affect it?

Am I using an *adequate base period* of statistics for my forecast? (The length of the base period should be at least twice that of the projection period to be statistically reasonable.)

When I feel that the forecast figures aren't right, do I let my *good judgment* take precedence over the mathematics? (Even the most elaborate, computerized system is no substitute for your specialized knowledge and understanding of cause-and-effect relationships in the market.)

Do my methods encourage an open-minded *contribution of judgment from my associates* and a realistic weighing and testing of alternatives?

Do they provide for regular *revisions and corrections* as new facts come to light?

Am I using *more than one forecasting technique* for greater reliability?

Do my associates—especially in the sales department—*understand the importance* of the forecast and how it can help their day-to-day operations?

Do I avoid *vague generalities?* (Too much hedging can make your report virtually useless.)

Do I give *assumptions* and how I arrived at them?

Do I give the *range of error?* (As observed in Section 3b, 100 percent accuracy in forecasting is a rarity and no reasonable executive expects it.)

4d   The Five Elements of Change

Before you can estimate what to expect in the future, you have to know what happened in the past. Studying your sales figures over past years, you'll undoubtedly find a pattern of ups and downs, or variations, brought about by the inexorable process of change. If it weren't for these, sales volume could be represented on a graph as a horizontal line and you could assume that sales volume would be the same for all future periods as it was in the past. There are many things that bring about change, some pushing up the sales figures, some pushing them down. But basically there are five types of change that the forecaster tries to identify and to estimate their effect on future sales. They are: (1) the long-term or "secular" trend, (2) the cycle, (3) seasonal fluctuations, (4) calendar variations, and (5) irregular occurrences. Here's how they are defined by the forecasting profession:

1. *Trend* is the long-term movement in a time series. Despite recessions and depressions (cycles), the American economy has shown an upward growth trend during its history. But some industries have declined over the long term, such as rail freight and hard coal mining. Others have declined and then staged a revival, such as wood stove manufacturing. If there is a trend up or down in your industry that is longer than one business cycle, what is the rate of growth or decline so you can incorporate this in your long-term forecasts? (In short-term forecasts, the trend is usually ignored by economists.)

2. *Cycles* are the wavelike fluctuations that flow above and below the long-term trend line. Sales cycles usually conform to the general business cycle, but some products or industries can have cycles of their own that are independent of business cycles. Nearly every business experiences these cycles. They are recurrent but not periodic, which makes them difficult to forecast. They range from one to ten years in length, with an average of four years.

3. *Seasonal fluctuations* are easier to predict in short-term forecasting because they are both recurrent and periodic, usually occurring in the same months every year and having to do with the weather, such as more coat sales in cold weather and more air conditioner sales in warm weather. Christmas buying, for instance, is a seasonal phenomenon that makes December a high sales month for many businesses, especially retail.

4. *Calendar variations* have to be taken into consideration when making monthly forecasts. These include:

the number of trading (or working) days in the month.
the number of Saturdays in the month (especially important to retail stores); Sundays, too, if stores are open.
Easter, which could come in either March or April.

5. *Irregular fluctuations* are those that can't be attributed to any of the four forces above. They are also called "random variables" and "irregular components." These are such things as strikes, embargoes, windfall sales, bad weather, fires, and floods. Such drastic disruptions usually can't be forecasted, but they could cause unrealistic changes in the averages. In such cases, it is best to substitute your estimate of what sales would have been for the period had the unusual event not occurred. Other irregular fluctuations with a certain amount of constancy are absorbed into the "moving average" (a basic statistical process that is explained in Section 8c).

4e   How To Measure Change

As we have pointed out, change is a basic ingredient of business—and forecasting. If it weren't for change, forecasts wouldn't be needed, for sales in the forthcoming period would be the same as sales in the previous period. So one of the first things the forecaster should learn is how change is measured.

It's really quite simple. Most statisticians follow the Census Bureau method, where change is measured in terms of the percentage of change from the preceding period. *Average change,* which is especially useful in comparing the rate of change of various products or product lines, is calculated with the familiar arithmetic mean, but without regard to plus or minus signs. For instance, if February's sales are 5 percent greater than January's, and March sales are down by 5 percent, the tendency would be to say that $+5$ and -5 equal zero change. But we know this isn't true because the change for each month was 5 percent, one plus and one minus.

This example shows how average change in a time series is arrived at, ignoring plus and minus signs.

	Sales	*% Change*
Jul.	1305	—
Aug.	1456	11.6
Sep.	1660	14.
Oct.	2040	22.9
Nov.	1980	− 2.9
Dec.	1850	− 6.5
Jan.	1760	− 4.9
		6)62.8
		10.46% (Average Change)

4f   In What Stage of Its Life-Cycle is Your Product?

Most products and product categories (and companies and industries too) go through a life-cycle consisting broadly of the growth period, stability or prosperity period, and the decline period. This is a fundamental concept in marketing as well as forecasting. It provides a framework within which the forecaster can anticipate the underlying forces that affect the product or product category and take steps to adjust to them.

Thus, in forecasting demand for your product, you should view your estimate according to the life-cycle stage of the product. Your first step should be to see if there have been any *changes in the slope and speed* of brand or product category life-cycles (see Figure 4.1). Is the decline or increase in sales due to short-term seasonal effects, to medium-term business cycle factors, to long-term changes in the company brand cycle, to actions by the competition, or to events beyond the company's control?

What *new strategies or changes* in existing strategies are required?

By keeping in mind the concept of the product life-cycle, you not only make more accurate forecasts but also better interpret, evaluate, and justify the data upon which the forecast is based (see Figure 4.2).

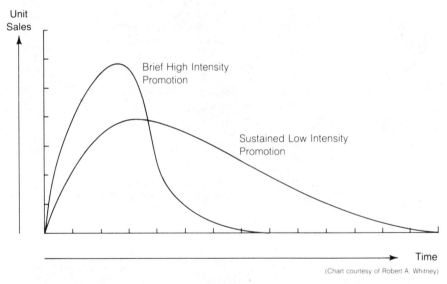

(Chart courtesy of Robert A. Whitney)

Figure 4.1. Relating Sales Potential to Time and Product Strategies

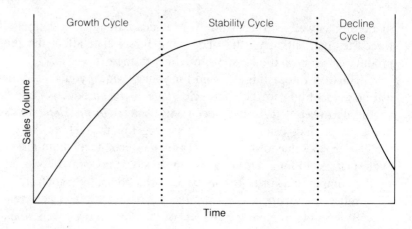

GROWTH CYCLE
    Advertising and promotion programs accelerate
    Increase in or redeployment of sales force
    New distribution methods sought
    New uses or markets for product sought or being introduced
    Is manufacturing keeping up with the demand?
    Profitability increasing as introductory expenses are amortized
STABILITY CYCLE
    Inventories about even with demand
    No expansion plans in the works
    No improvement in product contemplated
    Market seems to be reaching saturation point
    Profitability being maintained
DECLINE CYCLE
    Consumer demand declining
    Inventories being reduced
    Profitability declining
    Competition has better or less costly product
    If product category, slower products being phased out
    Customer returns greater
    Layoffs, reduction in expenses

Figure 4.2. Typical Life-Cycle of a Product

5

Forecasting with Executive Judgment

	All	*Small*	*Medium*	*Large*
Percentage of questionnaire respondents who use executive judgment exclusively or as major element in forecasting	77.%	78.8%	79.7%	72.6%

This is the original method of sales forecasting and still the most widely used, regardless of company size. More sophisticated methods, like time-series analysis and econometric regression, gain new converts every day as forecasters learn how to use them, aided by data-processing facilities. But the experienced executive's feel for the market—his/her ''educated hunches''—play a vital part in nearly every sales forecast, no matter how many mathematical techniques are also used.

A financial planning executive of a large liquor company told us: ''We use some of the most sophisticated forecasting methods known to man, keeping busy a battery of economists and statisticians. But we find there's no substitute in this business for the seasoned sales executive's 'seat-of-the-pants' intuition—the advantage of close personal contact with distributors and dealers—which we rely on in assessing our technically-derived forecasts.''

Judgmental forecasting is done in two ways: by one seasoned individual (usually in the small company) or by a group of individuals, sometimes called a "jury of executive opinion." The group approach, in turn, uses two methods: (1) key executives submit independent estimates without discussion and these are averaged into one forecast by the chief executive; (2) the group meets, each one presents his/her estimates, differences are resolved, and a consensus is reached. A rather interesting variation of the group method is the "prudent manager" exercise, where a panel of executives assumes the roles of members of the purchasing decision-making unit of a customer company, prudently assessing from available facts what the buyers are apt to want in the period ahead.

5a   When to Use Executive Judgment Forecasting

Executive judgment forecasting can be used:

When the executive or executives who forecast are experienced and have a good feel for the market and for customers' needs.

When you want to check on or fortify other methods of sales prediction you may be using.

When your budget for sales forecasting is limited.

When company or product is new and sales data are not available.

When your sales volume is fairly stable and the market well defined.

When the risk or consequences of serious error in forecasting is low.

5b   Disadvantages of Executive Judgment Forecasting

Yet, there are a number of pitfalls to executive judgment forecasting:

It relies entirely on *personal views* and may be mostly guesswork. Many companies try to meet this objection by giving their forecasting executives background information on the history of their sales and assumptions regarding the general business outlook.

It provides no way of *weighing and evaluating* individual opinions since there is usually no standard procedure established.

It may infringe too much on valuable executive time.

In group forecasting, *dominant individuals* usually determine group opinion. Group pressure for conformity may discourage the more timid members. This problem could be solved by use of the Delphi Technique, described below.

It tends to give *equal weight* to the predictions of the forecasters no matter how bad their estimates were in the past.

Since there's no established formula or methodology to follow, *new executives* could have difficulty in arriving at reasonable forecasts.

5c Could You Use the Delphi Technique?

Although less than 1 percent of our questionnaire respondents indicated that they've used the Delphi Technique or, for that matter, ever heard of it, some probably are using variations of it. This technique was developed by the Rand Corporation (and named after the oracle of Greek antiquity).

Essentially this is a method of minimizing some of the disadvantages of group forecasting mentioned above, mainly the influence of dominant individuals and the sacrifice of the more timid members to the group pressure to conform. It is used mostly to forecast new developments or technologies that could affect sales in the future.

Anonymity is achieved by using unsigned questionnaires. The results are summarized and fed back to members of the group, who are then asked if they wish to revise their predictions on the basis of the other estimates. This process might be repeated if there is a wide divergence of opinion. Finally, the group opinion is considered to be the statistical average of the final individual opinions.

At International Business Machines Corporation, this technique is used to estimate if a market is ready for certain new equipment. IBM's own experts, chosen for their diverse backgrounds and knowledge of the market, get together in some isolated spot so they can concentrate without interruption. Their anonymous estimates are quickly totaled by computer, a process which is repeated until consensus is reached.

Company Example
Bristol-Myers Products:
a Division of Bristol-Myers Company

Executive Judgment Guided by Statistical Information

Bristol-Myers is a good example of a large company that relies heavily on executive judgment to evaluate statistical data and the effectiveness of promotional plans and agree on the levels of forecasted sales. Their well-known products, such as Bufferin, Excedrin, and Ban deodorant, sell in highly competitive markets, so frequent changes in promotional expenditures and sales forecasts might have to be made to meet and beat the competition.

Once each quarter, department heads from Marketing, Sales, and Finance get together to discuss current product and business trends. After studying the mass of data from the company's statistical department and from outside sources, they then determine forecasted levels of sales for each brand and total sales by month, quarter, and year. The following information is compiled and used to achieve the most accurate forecast possible:

1. Trade Promotional Calendar
   a. Percent allowance offered to the trade by brand during the period.
   b. Number of times allowance will be offered during year.
   c. Expected trade participation and types of ads and displays they are expected to generate.
2. Consumer Promotional Calendar
   a. Coupon drops
   b. Media to be used—expected costs and results
   c. Refund offers
   d. Self-liquidators
   e. Rebates
   f. Theme or "umbrella" promotions scheduled
3. History
   a. Eight-year sales history of each brand.
   b. Percentage of yearly sales normally achieved by a brand during a given period (for instance, Brand X might have achieved 30% of its annual sales in the fourth quarter).
4. Market Share and Trend Information
   a. Data from Nielsen and Towne-Oller on competitive products, etc.
   b. Category trends
   c. Sub-category trends, such as percentages of total deodorant category done by roll-on, solid, and aerosol products.
   d. Brand trends

5. Price Changes
   a. When scheduled
   b. Prior sales levels before price increase
   c. Prior sales levels after price increase
6. McKinsey Forecasting Method

All of the above information is fed into the company's computers, using a program devised by McKinsey & Company to generate forecasts based on this data. The print-outs go to the department heads to guide them in preparing their forecasts by brand, month, quarter, and year. After they have done this, they meet and compare notes. Each brand is discussed and the agreed-upon level of forecasted sales is determined.

6

Estimates by the Sales Force

6a Why and When Sales Force Estimates Are Used

	All	Small	Medium	Large
We use sales force estimates	70.9%	57.7%	76.6%	78.3%
Our salespeople are formally polled on estimates of sales in their territories	38.4	34.6	34.3	46.2
Our sales managers or marketing directors make estimates rather than salespeople	20.4	15.3	25.	20.8
Both salespeople and sales managers are involved	59.4	50.	64.	64.1
We provide them with guidelines and past sales data to aid in their estimating	34.3	19.2	42.1	41.5

	All	Small	Medium	Large
Our distributors cooperate with us in providing estimates	8.3	3.8	7.8	13.2
Quotas for sales personnel are directly linked to their forecasts	26.1	17.3	32.8	28.3
We find that estimates by salespeople are usually:				
Underestimates	18.8	11.1	28.6	16.7
Overestimates	34.8	44.3	33.3	26.7
Pretty much on target	48.	44.4	42.9	56.7
We consider our salespeople's selling time too important to involve them in forecasting	1.5	0.	1.6	2.8

Heading the list in the tally on "What element of sales forecasting gives you the most trouble?" (Section 3i) was "inability of salespeople and their managers to judge their sales prospects accurately," mentioned by 33.2 percent of our respondents.

But the fact that 70.9 percent of our group use sales force estimates indicates that the practice is widespread nonetheless. Their reasoning is that sales personnel may be better positioned than others in the company to know what's going on in their respective territories and what the buying prospects of individual accounts should be. This is especially true when a company relies heavily on landing large proposals or bids, or where sales personnel are able to quiz customers or prospects about their probable buying plans.

In most cases, sales force estimates are used for relatively short periods ahead, such as the next quarter or the year to come, rather than for longer periods, when other methods would be more reliable. It is also common for sales personnel to be asked to rate the probability of closing each account on some scale agreed upon, such as 1 to 10, or a percentage.

A large sales agency reports: "Area managers (field sales people) submit case volume forecasts for each customer for each line they sell. Product managers submit case volume forecasts for each category of customer in each line. Both proceed independently. Differences are resolved in a joint review forecast meeting held by the chairman."

Union Carbide Chemicals and Plastics Division reports this procedure in obtaining sales force estimates:

Salespeople receive worksheets with historical sales data by market area, major customer, and major product in pound units.

After consulting with customers on their buying intentions, salespeople enter on worksheets annual pound volume forecast by market area, customer, and product, and forward this information to the marketing manager concerned with the particular product.

The marketing manager adjusts these estimates to conform to his/her own observations of the market and the reports of company research people.

The marketing manager and the product manager then estimate what the price per pound will be and figure the monthly dollar volume, with allowances made for seasonal variations observed in the historical sales data.

6b   Checklist for Getting Better Sales Force Estimates

Here is a checklist to use for improving your sales force estimates:

Has past experience shown that estimates by your sales force personnel are reliable?

Since some salespeople tend to overestimate and others to underestimate, do you keep a record of their accuracy in the past and adjust their estimates accordingly?

Do you provide salespeople with data to help them forecast, such as sales by product or customer for the year to date and for recent past years?

Do you have a form for salespeople to use in making their estimates? Examples of such forms are given in Figures 6.2, 6.3, and 6.4.

If yes, is the form uniform for all districts, with enough material to check for internal consistency?

Are instructions carefully and simply worded so that all elements are completely understood?

Is company policy made clear, such as that estimates should be made on the basis of existing product or service lines and current price structure with no speculation as to product or price changes?

Is it made clear to the salespeople that their quotas will not necessarily be based on their estimates, to offset the obvious possibilities for bias?

Have you considered offering a prize or bonus to the salesperson whose sales results come closest to his/her estimates? And perhaps a booby prize for the one furthest off the beam? (One company in our survey reports success with this idea.) See Section 6d for the pros and cons of such bonuses. For an example of how one company impresses on its salespeople the importance of accurate forecasting, see Figure 6.1 (p. 40).

6c   Problems Some Companies Encounter with Sales Force Estimates

Here are some typical problems encountered when estimates are provided by the sales force.

Salespeople are usually poor estimators, especially when it comes to identifying long-term trends.

Current conditions are apt to color their forecasts; they're optimistic when sales are good and pessimistic when sales are declining.

Sales managers are usually so concerned with administrative problems that they don't keep up with national or international developments and trends that could affect their sales. Even when they do keep up, they may not know how to translate them quantitatively for a sales forecast.

Salespeople may think it's smart to forecast low so their sales record looks good by comparison, or forecast high to impress headquarters with their enthusiasm. (Some companies keep a record of salespeople who habitually underestimate or overestimate and adjust their forecasts accordingly.)

Sales force estimating is time-consuming, especially as the company grows, and time might be better spent out in the field selling. (But only four out of 222 respondents in our survey expressed this opinion.)

Salespeople are usually pressed for time and interested only in immediate results, so they may not give forecasting questionnaires enough thought.

Name _____   Forecast of _____

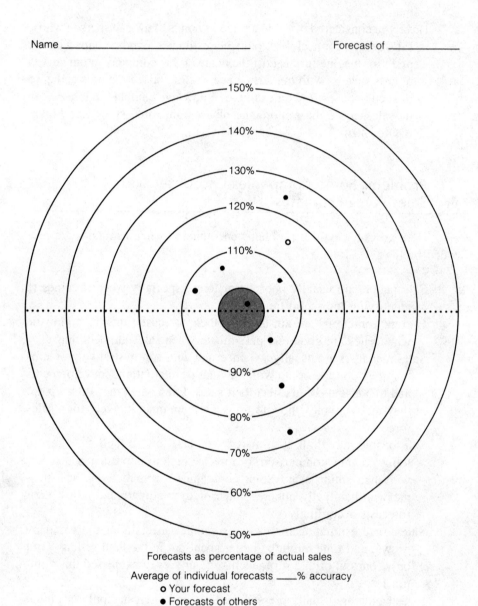

Forecasts as percentage of actual sales

Average of individual forecasts ____% accuracy
o Your forecast
● Forecasts of others

Adaptation of chart used by United-Carr Division of TRW Inc. to keep salespeople aware of their forecasting accuracy.

Figure 6.1. Your Forecast—How Close to the Bull's Eye?

Account Marketing Plan   _____ Date
Customer Name:*
Current status (continued)   _____ Salesman #

*If split account, indicate   % sales credited and only show that portion below.

Product (group by division)	19 ___ Sales $	Estimated 19 ___ Sales $**	Forecast 19 ___ Sales		Total Account Potential $
			$	Quantities	

**estimate based on latest available sales figures

page 2

M & T Chemicals, Inc.

Figure 6.2. Example of Forms Used to Get Sales Force Estimates

SUMMARY AND ANALYSIS OF TERRITORY

DISTRIBUTION
☐ SALESMAN
☐ BRANCH MANAGER
☐ DISTRICT MANAGER
☐ NEW YORK OFFICE CHEMICAL

SALESMAN _____
BRANCH _____
DISTRICT _____

DATE _____

CUSTOMERS		CLASSIFICATION OF ACCOUNTS $ PER YEAR	SALES						POTENTIAL			CALLS		
1	2	3	4	5	6	7	8		9	10		11	12	13
NUMBER	CODE		$ LAST YEAR	% OF TOTAL	$ FORECAST	% OF TOTAL	$ ESTIMATED		% OF TOTAL	AVERAGE $ POTENTIAL/ACCOUNT		NUMBER OF CALLS	% OF CALLS TO TOTAL	AVERAGE CALLS PER CUSTOMER
	A	$1-999												
	B	$1,000-4,999												
	C	$5,000-9,999												
	D	$10,000-24,999												
	E	$25,000-49,999												
	F	$50,000-UP												
		TOTAL												

PROSPECTS		CLASSIFICATION OF $ POTENTIAL					$ ESTIMATED		% OF TOTAL	AVERAGE $ POTENTIAL/ACCOUNT		NUMBER OF CALLS	% OF CALLS TO TOTAL	AVERAGE CALLS PER CUSTOMER
NUMBER	CODE		$ LAST YEAR	% OF TOTAL	$ FORECAST	% OF TOTAL								
	G	$1-999												
	H	$1,000-4,999												
	I	$5,000-9,999												
	J	$10,000-24,999												
	K	$25,000-49,999												
	L	$50,000-UP												
		TOTAL												
		GRAND TOTALS												

BRANCH & DISTRICT MANAGERS REMARKS

NEW YORK OFFICE REMARKS

McKesson Chemical Company

Figure 6.3. Example of Summary and Territory Analysis

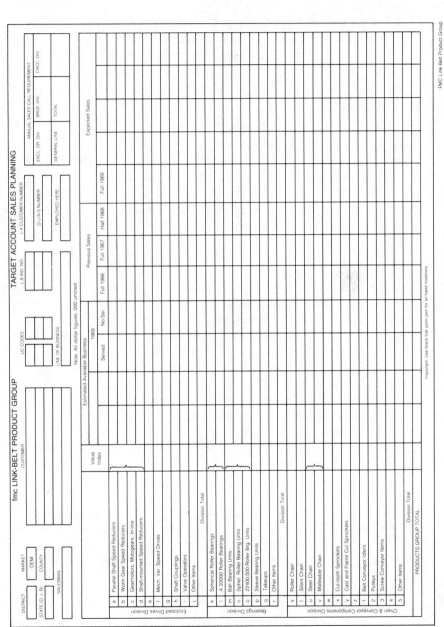

Figure 6.4. Example of Form Used to Get Sales Force Estimates

Company Example
Miracle Adhesives Corporation

Using Executive Judgment and Sales Force Estimates to Forecast Sales and Profitability in a Company with a Wide Range of Related Products

A good example of a company that uses basic methods to forecast sales and profitability for a wide variety of related products is the Miracle Adhesives Corporation of Bellmore, New York. Manufacturing and selling over 500 items in the field of adhesives, sealants, and coatings, accurate forecasting is important to help protect profitability and to maintain inventories without overstocking or understocking, according to Charles R. Van Anden, executive vice-president.

Sales of this small-to-medium-sized company are made by 11 staff salespeople and 33 manufacturer's representatives. They sell to the construction industry and to the retail trade through distributors and mass merchandisers. Forecasts are made by the trade serviced.

Here is their forecasting procedure:

1. In July of each year, Miracle's Data Processing Department prints a three-year sales history and a projection for the coming year. The projection is based on historical movement of the product. It is broken down by Division (Commercial, Consumer, and Private Label) as well as by Department (Ceramic Tile and Flooring, Building Supply, Insulation, Home Products, Drywall, and Industrial). Figures for total dollar sales, total poundage, and gross profit are given *by month*, reflecting any seasonality.

2. The Data Forecast is given to each of the Divisional Sales Managers. After review, the DSMs send to their eleven territory salespeople a print-out of their sales for the past three years, but minus the forecast for the coming year. They review their customers and prospects and estimate what they believe they will achieve during the coming year. This again is done by the month.

The company's 33 manufacturer's representatives are not involved in the forecasting process. "These people are free agents," says Mr. Van Anden, "and they just won't do the research and paperwork involved in forecasting." But each rep receives a print-out with the information concerning his or her operation contained in step number one, including the company's estimate of the rep's sales for the forthcoming year.

3. After all salespeople have completed their forecasts, results are submitted to the Divisional Sales Manager, who reviews them in the light of the data forecast, market trends, economic conditions, and new market programs scheduled to be introduced during the coming year. Adjustments are made and this final forecast is submitted to the Vice-President of Sales and Marketing. After a thorough review, a final forecast is approved.

An unusual feature of Miracle Adhesives forecast is the incorporation of estimates of gross profit margins to be expected for each customer and group of products. These are compared with the profit margins of the previous year. These figures are important to show the salesperson's ability to maintain the company's price structure in the face of competition, state of the economy, and other problems.

Every month, an analysis is made of each territory. This review graphically shows any trouble spots, indicating the volume each customer is doing, the new customers obtained, and whether or not the expected gross profit margins are being maintained.

What have been the company's main problems in arriving at accurate forecasts? The biggest one over the past five years (1977 to 1982), according to Mr. Van Anden, has been the turmoil in the petrochemical industry caused by the oil-energy crisis. Other problems listed in order of their importance have been trying to gauge the condition of the economy, inability of salespeople to judge their customers and prospects accurately, changes in government policies or regulations, influence of the weather, effectiveness of advertising and sales promotion, and actions of competitors. Other forecasting problems he cites are a lack of reliable industry data and inability to find a good economic indicator in addition to housing starts.

Since Miracle's forecasts rely heavily on sales force estimates, the familiar "inability of salespeople to judge their customers and prospects accurately" has been a problem to the company's management. Sales force estimates have tended to be too high, making it necessary for management to discount their estimates by the amount of their overoptimism in the past. In an attempt to solve this problem, the company has devised an incentive program whereby 75 percent of the salespeople's bonus is keyed to how close their estimates come to actual sales. They achieve maximum bonus only if their sales are within 95 percent and 105 percent of forecast. (For further details on this program, along with the potential hazards of similar programs, see Section 6d.)

M I R A C L E   A D H E S I V E S   C O R P O R A T I O N

SALES ANALYSIS BY SALESPERSON AND BY DEPARTMENT

* COMMERCIAL *   40   S BAXTER

AUG 1982

P O U N D S

DEPARTMENTS	AUG 1981	AUG 1982	% DIFF	AUG 1982 QUOTA	YTD 1981	YTD 1982	% DIFF	YTD 1982 QUOTA
10 INSULATION	6.865	11.823	41.94		51.915	49.992	3.85-	
11 INSULATION	126		100.00-		1.261	184	585.33-	
40 TILE	11.660	25.097	53.54		363.807	249.185	46.00-	
41 TILE			100.00-		14.466	6.631	111.77-	
44 TILE		11.150	100.00			89.954	100.00	
50 BUILDING SUPPLIES	10.004	654-	629.66		35.477	23.735	49.47-	
51 BUILDING SUPPLIES			100.00-		162		100.00-	
60 HOME PRODUCTS		755	100.00-		4.239	3.263	29.91-	
70 INDUSTRIAL			100.00-		2.243	3.870	42.04	
71 INDUSTRIAL		620	100.00-		146	1.673	91.27	
80 DRYWALL	104.866	170.058	38.34		1.070.522	942.641	13.57-	
81 DRYWALL			100.00-			65	100.00	
TOTALS	133.521	218.849	38.99	217.200	1.544.238	1.371.393		1.846.200

S A L E S

DEPARTMENTS	AUG 1981	AUG 1982	% DIFF	AUG 1982 QUOTA	YTD 1981	YTD 1982	% DIFF	YTD 1982 QUOTA
10 INSULATION	3.832	12.042	68.18		39.489	43.954	10.16	
11 INSULATION	271		100.00-		3.614	592	510.47-	
40 TILE	4.130	11.264	63.33		131.458	102.359	28.43-	
41 TILE			100.00-		5.391		100.00-	
44 TILE		1.196	100.00			2.847	89.36	
50 BUILDING SUPPLIES	7.320	510-	535.29		27.397	11.869	100.00	
51 BUILDING SUPPLIES			100.00-		108	21.162	23.46	
60 HOME PRODUCTS		744	100.00-		3.977	3.223	23.39-	
70 INDUSTRIAL			100.00-		3.438	4.416	22.15	
71 INDUSTRIAL		1.940	100.00-		452	6.384	92.92	
80 DRYWALL	42.098	70.394	40.20		414.697	369.998	6.33-	
81 DRYWALL			100.00-			180	100.00	
TOTALS	57.651	97.070		57.653	630.021	586.984	7.33-	630.028

Figure 6.5. Miracle Adhesives Corporation   1982

Should Salespeople be Paid Bonuses for
6d ⋅Sharper Forecasts?

Since most companies use sales force estimates as an important element of their sales forecasts, the question many forecasting executives are asking is, "How can we get salespeople to come up with more accurate estimates?" taking into account the previously-cited tendency of most of them either to underestimate or overestimate.

Should they receive a bonus based on how close their estimates come to actual sales? Where this is done, the usual policy is to pay salespeople the maximum bonus if their sales fall between, say, 95 percent and 105 percent of forecast.

This device seems pretty simple in theory. But in practice it could present problems that tax the ingenuity of the smartest compensation specialist. Here are some of the things that you have to consider:

If your factory production is based on sales force estimates, accurate forecasts are important to prevent profit-robbing excess inventories or stock-outs.

BUT

Are you putting an artificial cap on sales and profits by encouraging diminished sales effort once the forecast has been surpassed?

Since the chances are that some territories might not achieve their forecasts, you might want a salesperson in another territory to greatly surpass forecast sales to make up the difference. The forecast-geared bonus then acts as a disincentive.

If your company has more than one product, the forecast-based bonus could discourage the salesperson from pushing certain products that are most profitable to the company.

Salespeople are apt to look upon such a bonus plan as a way of limiting their income, since a reduced incentive on over-forecast sales that are presumably the most difficult to make and most profitable to the company would seem rather illogical to them.

Arguing that the easier the forecast to achieve the greater the reward, the salesperson might be encouraged to set a low estimate that could defeat extra sales effort, increase compensation costs, and reduce profitable returns.

What's the best way to solve this puzzle? Compensation specialist John K. Moynahan, vice-president of Towers, Perrin, Forster, and Crosby, suggests a bonus arrangement worked out "to ensure that maximum income can be achieved only by satisfying some combination of difficulty of forecast, performance vs. forecast, and accuracy of forecast." Writing in *Sales and Marketing Management,* he suggests that such a bonus program would have to include the following elements:

> A forecast bonus that becomes more generous as the size of the forecast increases, in addition to varying, of course, by the accuracy of the forecast.
> A bonus for exceeding forecasted sales.
> A bonus for increasing sales over the prior year.

"To place different priorities on different product groups," Mr. Moynahan says, "the company would probably have to index the calculation of sales to reflect the relative priority of (and hence reward for) each product group. Then management would have to undertake considerable mathematical modeling to ensure the proper balance between the rewards for forecast accuracy and the rewards for difficulty of forecast. Only under such a system can a company have any realistic hope of using sales incentive compensation to improve forecasting."

Company Example
Rewarding Forecast Accuracy
at Miracle Adhesives Corporation

One company that reports success with a bonus system for rewarding accurate estimates is the Miracle Adhesives Corporation of Bellmore, New York (see outline of their forecasting procedures on page 44).

"Manufacturing and selling over five hundred items presents a real inventory problem," says Charles R. Van Anden, executive vice-president. "So it's vital for us to estimate sales potential as accurately as possible. The salesperson's bonus for accuracy is an important tool in accomplishing this."

Miracle's sales incentive program is based on the following factors:

1. Level of sales achieved prior year in poundage.
2. Sales forecast (by poundage).
3. Gross profit level of prior year's sales.
4. Forecasted gross profit.

Using the salesperson's prior year sales and comparing it to forecasted sales, a volume base is agreed upon at which point incentive will start to be earned. A fixed percentage is paid on all sales after the sales surpass the base figure. Once sales reach 95 percent of forecast, the percentage paid doubles. It stays at that figure until sales reach 105 percent of forecast, at which point the incentive drops to the first level.

For example: (Salesperson A)

1980 sales	10,940,000 pounds
1981 forecast	12,900,000 pounds
1981 base	11,935,000 pounds
1980 Gross Profit	37%
1981 Gross Profit	37%

The base is determined as the amount necessary to cover costs and return a profit to the company. Incentive payments are made on all sales over this base, as follows:

1 percent for all sales over base figure and below 95 percent of forecast

2 percent for all sales between 95 and 105 percent of forecast

1 percent for all sales over 105 percent of forecast

Gross profit on the salesperson's sales is also an important factor in incentive earnings. The plan is weighted to make the penalty for price-cutting greater than the reward for selling above the gross profit target. For each half-percentage point drop in gross profit, the salesperson is penalized 15 percent of earned incentive. For each increase of a half-percent in gross profit, the incentive is increased 10 percent.

Figure 6.6 shows how Miracle's sales incentive program worked out for Salesperson A in 1981, according to these specifications:

(in pounds)

	1st Qtr.	2nd Qtr.	3rd Qtr.	4th Qtr.	Total
1980 sales	2,410,000	2,730,000	2,960,000	2,840,000	10,940,000
1981 forecast	2,680,000	3,170,000	3,580,000	3,470,000	12,900,000
1981 sales	2,550,000	3,240,000	3,610,000	3,715,000	13,115,000
Base	2,530,000	2,905,000	3,300,000	3,200,000	11,935,000
Selling price per pound	.43	.45	.42	.44	

"At first, our incentive plan may seem a bit complicated," says Mr. Van Anden. "But it doesn't take long for the salespeople to understand it and to see the logic of it from our point of view and theirs. So far, we've had no problems. And they really concentrate on getting that extra 1 percent bonus for forecasting realistically. Which, of course, is so important to us in planning our production and servicing."

Figure 6.6 Miracle's Salesman Incentive Program (Salesperson A)

Quarter	1981 Sales over Base Figure below 95% of Forecast	Selling Price Per Pound	Sales over Base × Selling Price Per Pound	INCENTIVE RATE			Gross Profit	Total
				Up to 95% of Forecast of Sales over Base = 1%	From 95%–105% of Forecast of Sales over Base = 2%	Over 105% of Forecast of Sales over Base = 1%		
1st	2,550,000 lbs. −2,530,000 lbs. = 20,000 lbs.	.43	20,000 lbs. × .43 = $ 8,600	$ 86.00			(37%)	$ 86.00
2nd	3,011,500 lbs. −2,905,000 lbs. = 106,500 lbs.	.45	106,000 lbs. × .45 = $47,925	$479.25	$2,056.50		½% increase earns 10% (37½%)	$2,789.33
3rd	3,401,000 lbs. −3,300,000 lbs. = 101,000 lbs.	.42	101,000 lbs. × .42 = $42,420	$424.20	$1,755.60		1% decrease penalty 30% (36%)	$1,525.86
4th	3,296,500 lbs. −3,200,000 lbs. = 96,000 lbs.	.44	96,000 lbs. × .44 = $42,240	$422.40	$3,053.60	$314.60	½% decrease penalty 15% (36½%)	$3,222.01
								$7,623.20

6e   Using "Expected Value" to Measure the Potential of an Account

When estimating potential sales for specific accounts, the sales force might use a formula developed by Dr. Robert F. Vizza, Dean of the School of Business, Manhattan College.*

Having determined the total potential market for your product or service through trade association or trade publication estimates, Input-Output Tables (see Section 10c), and other methods, you then estimate what your share of that market should be. The estimate of what you can reasonably expect is called Expected Value. Expected Value is calculated with this formula:

$$\text{Market Potential} \times \text{Estimated Share} \times \text{Probability} = \text{Expected Value}$$
$$\text{M.P.} \times \text{E.S.} \times \text{P} = \text{E.V.}$$

The estimated share and probability of realizing that share of an account's potential depend upon many variables:

1. Present share of that potential.
2. Degree and kind of competition.
3. Product, price, and service differentials with competitors.
4. Relationships with the account.

Assigning the estimated share and probability figures represents a judgmental decision by the salesperson or the manager.

Finally, some convenient system of account classification is necessary in order to group accounts by potential. Designating categories with a simple A, B, C, D, E rating is a commonly used approach. Figure 6.7 illustrates a total approach to account analysis:

Column 1 shows the account name and number (necessary if sales analysis is computerized).
Column 2 is the classification of that account by potential (A, B, C, etc.).

---

*From "Time and Territorial Management for the Salesmen," by Dr. Robert F. Vizza. A research study for the Sales Executives Club of New York, 1971.

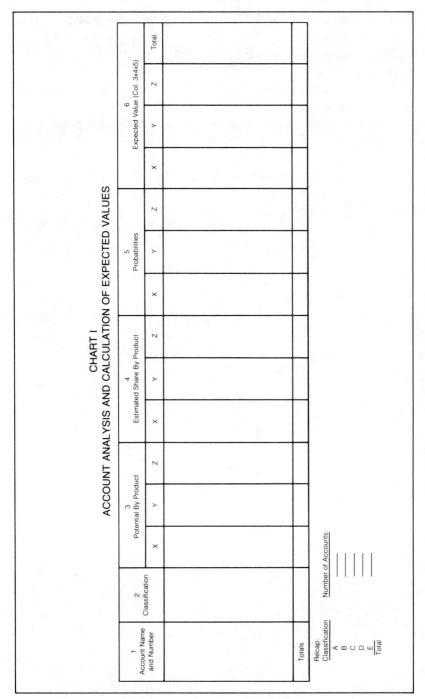

Figure 6.7. Account Analysis and Calculation of Expected Values

Column 3 shows the potential of the account for each product (X, Y, Z, etc.) in the mix.

Column 4 shows the estimated share of that potential that the firm can reasonably expect.

Column 5 is the probability of getting the estimated share of the potential (expressed as a percentage).

Column 6 is the Expected Value of that account for each product, and total value.

Such information is vital not only to the sales forecaster but also to the sales manager in determining the resources of time and effort and money required to change potential into reality.

7

Polling the End Users

7a How It Works

Polling is usually done by companies with a well-defined or limited market, principally in the industrial field. Customers and prospects are asked to indicate their buying intentions for the year ahead. Polling is usually done by the sales organization. Some companies with a broader market take only a sample of the market.

7b Advantages Cited

Gives a good feel of the market and its needs.
Keeps you abreast of competition.
Provides clues to new products and new uses for existing products.
Indicates size of customer inventories.
Shows where additional advertising, promotion, and personal selling pressure may be needed.

7c Disadvantages Cited

Product users may be too numerous, or too hard and expensive to locate, even using a sample.

Many of those reached might not know, or be unwilling to reveal, their buying intentions. Or, having stated their intentions, they might change their minds either about purchase or time of purchase.

In the case of broad markets, the method requires very expert sampling, with repeated polling at frequent intervals to check changes in opinions or intentions.

Estimates based on polling may be more a reflection of guesses by product users than informed judgment in the field.

Distributors and dealers may not be willing to take on the extra work of tracing and questioning customers or potential customers.

7d Getting Distributor Cooperation in Forecasting

Our study showed that only 8.3 percent of the companies sampled get cooperation from their distributors in forecasting sales. The reasons given for this are what might be expected: distributors are usually an independent lot; they're too busy to do adequate customer polling, they resent having more paperwork, and so on. But some companies have taken the trouble to devise special forecasting and marketing programs with their distributors—and to prove to them that cooperation means profits.

Company Example
Aro Corporation

An Ideal Manufacturer-Distributor Relationship

One company reported to have considerable success in working with its distributors on forecasts is the Aro Corporation, a large manufacturer of air tools, fluid power handling equipment, and related products, with a field force of 112 salespersons. Every six months, the sales managers sit down with their key distributors to draw up forecasts and specific marketing plans for the next six months.

According to an account in *Sales and Marketing Management* by Sally Scanlon,* the company provides the following to help them in their planning:

A territorial performance profile, which shows the annual distributor sales in each manager's territory over a four-year period.

A distributor's performance profile that shows sales for each distributor by product group for the same period. Each profile is accompanied by graphs comparing annual volume growth with real growth (subtracting the inflation factor of Aro's price increases from sales volume).

Marketing plan outlines

Blank planning calendars

The marketing plan outlines aid the company person and the distributor to work out specific sales goals by month, by product group, and by key account for the six months ahead. They also agree on a detailed plan for reaching those goals. It consists of:

Dollar sales goals to be aimed at.

What products and what dollar volume the distributor plans to sell to key accounts.

Which distributor salesperson will be responsible for those accounts.

Dates on which the Aro sales manager will make joint calls with the distributor's salespeople.

Dates of sales meetings to be arranged for the distributor, plus the topics to be discussed.

Distributor plans to participate in trade shows that will include Aro products.

*Summarized by permission from *Sales & Marketing Management* magazine, August 20, 1979. Copyright 1979.

Field sales seminars and headquarters training programs that the distributor's sales and service people will attend.

Dates for mailings and other promotional activities the distributor will use to support Aro sales.

Inventory to be carried, including specific product numbers, dollar values, and delivery schedules.

When the plan is agreed upon and completed, it goes without delay to the appropriate marketing manager, who reviews it and, upon approval, incorporates it in the division marketing plan for each territory. The general marketing manager then approves all the plans and coordinates them in the overall marketing program.

When the distributor cooperation plan was first devised and tested, there was the usual fear that the distributors would rebel at all the paperwork involved. But Aro has built so many benefits into the program that the distributors seem to welcome the opportunity to get involved in Aro's planning. They feel that the company considers them partners in marketing and will back them up all the way. For instance, the Aro sales training programs are considered by the distributors as second to none.

Aro believes that the most important benefit it gets from the program is the distributors' commitment to clearly defined goals. This the company reinforces with a balanced and aggressive marketing plan to make those goals a reality.

Company Example
Agfa-Gevaert Rex

*Using Analysis of Markets and Company Resources to Forecast Sales
in a Highly Specialized Field*

Agfa-Gevaert Rex, headquartered in White Plains, New York, is a subsidiary of Agfa-Gevaert, Inc., of Teterboro, New Jersey, the large photographic supply manufacturer and distributor. Agfa-Gevaert Rex handles distribution of the company's medical X-ray products in the United States.

According to Robert A. M. Coppenrath, president and general manager of the parent company, Agfa-Gevaert Rex uses a forecasting system that involves the identification and assessment of both external and internal factors that are judged to affect directly or indirectly Agfa-Gevaert's position in the medical X-ray film market.

In addition, "seat of the pants" interpretation of the impact of forces at work in the market, plus knowledge of how the market has behaved in the past, play a key role in forecasting, once the "recognition factors" have been determined. These recognition factors are:

External Factors—Regional Analysis of Markets

1. Sales data for each market region—Northeast, Central, Southeast, Midwest, Northwest, and Southwest—collected and analyzed.
2. Current and projected economic conditions—estimate of their effect on health care systems in these markets.
3. Capital investment in new X-ray equipment—what will be the increase in X-ray materials usage.
4. Make-up of user population. Effect of union and other third-party medical insurance plans upon local health care systems. Effect of population aging on X-ray usage.
5. Government medical policies current and planned and effect on hospital reimbursement systems.
6. Regional analysis of competitive activity.
   Changes in competitors' manpower.
   Changes in competitors' market concentration.
   Regional introduction of innovative competitive products.
7. Regional differences in adapting new systems and techniques, such as higher number of CAT scan units in South Florida than in the state of Georgia.

Internal Factors—Company Fiscal Policy and Strategic Market Planning

Manpower Planning:

Budgeting: How will mandated limits on expenditures affect expansion of markets and territories?

Sales personnel turnover: How will this affect the maintenance of current volume as well as the securing of new business?

Reassignment of territories: What sales increases can be expected from this?

Assessment of new skills to meet technology changes: What effect will the program of upgrading technical selling skills have on sales in the coming period(s)?

Product Line Planning—Analyzing Current Product Line to Determine Competitive Position

Availability of new products during forecast period and impact upon annual sales. Emphasis placed on replacement of obsolete parts.

Competitiveness of current product line with consideration given to obsolescence of certain products during forecast period.

Anticipated delivery problems based on factory performance history. How effective will new distribution policies be?

Interchangeability of existing and new products with competitive systems.

Impact of Major New Contracts

The forecast must anticipate the impact of large, new pieces of business that the sales staff is currently working on or that might come as windfalls. What is important here for forecasting and inventory control is not the contract award date but the actual product delivery dates. Also considered in the forecast must be the carryover factor of contracts awarded on the customer's fiscal year basis, which might not coincide with Agfa-Gevaert Rex's budget and sales forecast period.

This is but one of six different sales forecasts made by Agfa-Gevaert for its varied product lines. Forecasts are made annually, with semiannual updates. All executive personnel, product managers, production managers, and field sales managers receive the annual forecasts five months before the beginning of the forecast period. Over the period of 1977 to 1981, forecasting accuracy has been between 95 percent and 99 percent.

Salespeople and district sales managers are polled for their estimates of future sales in the respective territories. They receive print-outs of past sales data

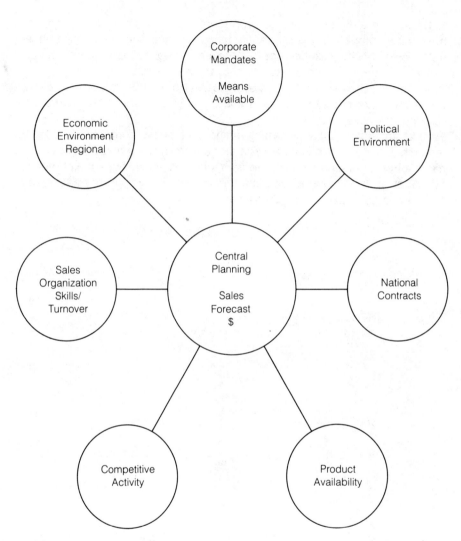

Figure 7.1. Agfa–Gevaert Rex Sales Forecasting Determining Factors

to help guide them in coming up with more realistic estimates. Even so, as in most other companies, the sales force tends to overestimate, so management routinely adjusts their exuberance to more realistic levels, based upon past experience. Salespeople's quotas are keyed to these forecasts.

Agfa-Gevaert also gets good cooperation from its distributors in providing estimates of their future purchases and possible changes in the demand for certain products.

In an industry that is fast-changing and highly competitive, constant research is necessary to keep abreast and ahead of the market. Agfa-Gevaert has its own continuing research program, aided by an outside market research firm. They are able to get reliable statistics on their industry from trade associations, trade publications, and the Department of Commerce.

8

Forecasting with
Time-Series Analysis

8a What is Time-Series Analysis?

Time-Series Analysis has long been a standard tool of the sales fore-caster. Knowing how it works is important to understanding the more tech-nical methods of forecasting that we review in the rest of this report.

To begin with, a time series is any set of related figures arranged by specific points in time. For instance, your total dollar sales for each year over the past ten years is a time series. So is your sales by month for the past year.

Forecasters analyze these figures to try to come up with a trend* line that can be projected into the future. Since most companies' past sales, plotted on a graph, show considerable ups and downs, the forecaster tries to smooth out these variations to produce the trend line on the graph. This is done by the simple process known as the moving average, which is ex-plained and illustrated in Section 8c.

The forecaster also looks for cyclical variations, identified as regular long-term ups and downs in the sales curve, and seasonal variations (in short-term forecasts of less than a year). Also noted are irregular variations, caused by such things as unusual weather, strikes, embargoes, etc. If the forecaster feels that any of these variations is apt to recur in the period being forecast, their average effect on sales is calculated and this is worked into the forecast equation:

*The term ''trend'' is used here to denote the direction of recent events and should not be confused with long-term or ''secular'' trend. (See Section 4c.)

Sales = Trend × Cyclical Variation × Irregular Variation × Seasonal Variation (if forecasting within the year)

8b   Making a Simple Time-Series Trend Graph

The elements of simple time-series analysis can best be visualized by graphing company sales history in this manner:

1. List your sales volume over a period of time—say, ten years or twelve months.
2. Plot these figures on a piece of graph paper, putting x's where time and volume figures intersect.
3. Draw a line connecting the x's. This is your actual performance line.
4. Do a moving average of your figures by, say, three-period segments, for each segment dropping the first period of the preceding segment and adding the next period (see Figure 8.1, page 65). Average each segment (divide totals by 3). Plot each average as a dot on your graph.
5. Draw a dotted line (or a different color line) connecting the dots. This is your trend line.
6. To determine your forecast, take your latest moving average and add to it (or subtract) the differences between the last two moving averages multiplied by 2 (subtract if the difference is negative). In our illustration, 373 is added to twice 23, totaling 419. Plot this as a point on your graph and extend the trend line.

8c   The Moving Average Explained

For those unfamiliar with the moving average process, here's how it works in Figure 8.1:

1969 – 125	1970 – 200	1971 – 160	
1970 – 200	1971 – 160	1972 – 250	
1971 – 160	1972 – 250	1973 – 300	and so on
total 485	total 610	total 710	
÷ 3 = 161.7	÷ 3 = 203.3	÷ 3 = 236.7	

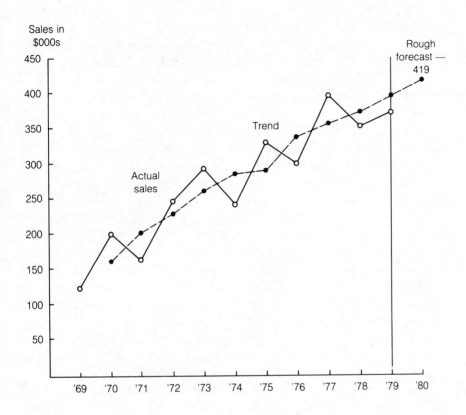

Year	Sales $000	3-year moving total	3-yr. moving average (trend)	Trend difference from last period
1969	125			
1970	200	485	161.7	
1971	160	610	203.3	41.6
1972	250	710	236.7	33.4
1973	300	800	266.7	30.
1974	250	875	291.7	25.
1975	325	875	291.7	0.
1976	300	1025	341.7	50.
1977	400	1050	350.	18.3
1978	350	1120	373.	23.
1979	375			
1980ʹ	Year to be forecast			

Figure 8.1. Sales History Showing Growth Trend and Up-and-Down Cycles

You can use any reasonable number of time periods in each segment of your moving average. If we had used five years instead of three, the effect would have been to bring the trend line closer to a straight line, further ironing out those ups and down in the actual sales line. But when sales show as much fluctuation as the mythical company in our example, the shorter moving average segment better reflects more recent conditions.

Also, in graphing your moving averages, it is important to plot the average for each period on the center year, month, or week that the average represents. This is called "centering." For this reason, it is advisable to have an odd number of periods in your moving average, if possible. (See more on centering in Section 9b, "Going Back to Census I—an Exercise.")

This method of forecasting works best when sales data gradually increases or decreases. When unusual, nonrecurring events inflate or deflate the moving average (such as a strike or an unexpected windfall sale), upward or downward adjustments of values should be made to allow for this. One way to do this would be to "adjust" the sales figure for the unusual year to an amount that normally would have been anticipated. This would keep the average within an acceptable range of the actual sales figures.

An interesting use of the moving average method is cited by the New York Telephone Company, which employs this technique to forecast cash collection intervals on coin telephones. A twelve-month moving average is used and the data is exponentially smoothed to account for seasonal variations. A high value is placed on the most recent collection experience. The same method is used to forecast general revenue data.

8d   Short-Term Forecasting

This same moving average method is used, of course, in short-term forecasting. Most companies, whether they deal in a product or a service, consider three months ahead a good short-term forecasting span, since it corresponds roughly to the typical delivery cycle.

Because it deals with company operations in the immediate future, it is commonly called the *operating forecast*. It is important in planning such activities as production, purchasing, and pricing and in directing sales effort. In this type of forecast, seasonal and short-term random elements are important. In which months are sales affected by the weather? Which months have holidays that boost sales, such as Christmas, Easter, or Thanksgiving? How will the number of trading days or the number of Saturdays in the month affect sales? Do you have vacation shutdowns? If so, are they regular from year to year?

Cycles too can have a bearing on short-term forecasts. Is business generally on an upswing or downswing? Is your particular industry growing or shrinking? Does your product or service have a cycle independent of the business or industry cycle—such as a "hot" item whose sales are rising in spite of a downward trend in the industry or the economy?

8e   Advantages of Time-Series or Trend and Cycle Analysis

It's fairly simple to understand and apply.

It forces a regular appraisal of trends, cycles, and seasonal elements that affect the sales picture.

It provides guidelines for judgmental forecasts.

It is "the beginning of the forecasting effort," according to some forecasting specialists. It gives the forecaster a picture of the sales environment he is responsible for planning.

8f   Disadvantages of Time-Series Analysis

There's a danger of projecting trends and cycles mechanically without considering the impact of possible changes in the future. This can be minimized by combining the method with executive judgment and more sophisticated methods discussed later on in this report.

Averaging the effect of trends and cycles over an extended period gives no special emphasis to the current ones, which are more apt to be present in the near future. Greater weight should be given to the most recent sales history.

In many companies, sales figures might have to be extended back over 20 or 30 years to prove cyclical activity. Often no attempt is made to separate trend and cycle. They are considered as one component after seasonal and irregular factors have been smoothed out by averaging (as in our simplified example above).

The Moving Average and Rate-of-Change Analysis
8g   at Cahners

In the previous example, we saw how a moving average could "smooth" our time series to enable us to plot a trend line. Another use of the moving average (or moving total) is to pinpoint shifting rates of change in sales. In forecasting advertising sales for each of its many trade publications, Cahners Publishing Company keeps track of these shifts and compares them to shifts in certain leading economic indicators that they have found to lead the business cycle by a number of months—an interval that usually remains quite constant. A composite of these leading economic indicators, called the Cahners Early Warning Indicator, is said to run 11 months ahead of Gross National Product and most current indexes.

Table A   Sales or Leading Indicator Series

	Year C-3	Year C-2	Year C-1	Current Year C
Jan.	108.7	122.2	125.4	113.7
Feb.	110.0	123.4	124.6	111.2
Mar.	111.6	123.7	124.7	110.0
Apr.	113.2	124.1	124.9	109.9
May	113.8	124.9	125.7	110.1
June	114.4	125.6	125.8	110.9
July	115.1	126.7	125.5	111.5
Aug.	116.3	126.5	125.2	114.0
Sept.	117.6	126.8	125.6	116.0
Oct.	119.2	127.0	124.8	116.6
Nov.	120.2	127.5	121.7	116.8
Dec.	121.1	126.5	117.9	

Here are the basic steps in the Cahners method:

First step: List the monthly figures, using either actual or index values for sales or the leading indicator series for each month for the current year to date and, say, the three preceding years (see Table A).

Table B   12-month Moving Totals

	Year C-3	Year C-2	Year C-1	Current Year C
Jan.		1394.7	1508.1	1480.1
Feb.		1408.1	1509.3	1466.7
Mar.		1420.2	1510.3	1452.0
Apr.		1431.1	1511.1	1437.0
May		1442.2	1511.9	1421.4
June		1453.4	1512.1	1406.5
July		1465.0	1510.9	1392.5
Aug.		1475.2	1509.6	1381.3
Sept.		1484.4	1508.4	1371.7
Oct.		1492.2	1506.2	1363.5
Nov.		1499.5	1500.4	1358.6
Dec.	1381.2	1504.9	1491.8	

Second step: Create another list with the 12-month moving totals of the first list, starting with the earliest year. In Table B, 1381.2 is the total of the figures from January of C-3 to December of C-3, 1394.7 is the total of figures from February of C-3 to January of C-2, and so on. A quick way to do this in calculations after the first one is to subtract the first figure (here 108.7) from the total (1381.2) and add the next one (here 122.2).

Table C   12-month Rates of Change

	Year C-3	Year C-2	Year C-1	Current Year C
Jan.			108.1	98.1
Feb.			107.2	97.1
Mar.			106.3	96.1
Apr.			105.6	95.0
May			104.8	94.0
June			104.0	93.0
July			103.1	92.1
Aug.			102.3	91.5

	Year C-3	Year C-2	Year C-1	Current Year C
Sept.			101.6	90.9
Oct.			100.9	90.5
Nov.			100.1	90.5
Dec.		109.0	99.1	

Third step: To determine the monthly rates of change, you divide each 12-month total by the corresponding figure for the same month the year before and multiply the result by 100. For instance, the 12-month rate of change for January of the current year was:

$$\frac{1480.1}{1508.1} \times 100 = 98.1$$

Cahners then plots these rate-of-change figures on a graph, which shows visually the cyclical patterns that are familiar to many businesses as well as Cahners' advertising sales. Based on their observations of curves in the past, the forecasters sometimes assume that the span of time between the last high or low in their sales series will be about the same as that of the leading indicator. (For more on economic indicators, see Section 10.)

They also use the rate-of-change figures to predict sales for some near future month or quarter year (averaging the values for the quarter-year period).

Accuracy of the Cahners method is quite remarkable. Its various forecasts for recent years are reported to be within .23% and 3.8% of actual sales.*

8h   Forecasting from Initial Orders (for Seasonal Businesses)

If you're in a seasonal line of business selling, let's say, to wholesalers or retailers, another technique of time-series analysis—*initial order forecasting*—could be of interest to you. By analyzing the initial orders you received last year, you can develop a pretty good forecast of the initial orders you'll receive this coming year.

*Tables and data used in the above illustration have been adapted from the Cahners manual, "How to Make Early Warning Forecasts," and from the Conference Board's publication, "Sales Forecasting."

Jantzen Inc., a swimsuit and sportswear manufacturer, uses a method described by Carl Vreeland in the April 1963 *Journal of Marketing* and updated in the Conference Board's forecasting study.

They use this formula:

$$
\begin{array}{ccc}
\text{Forecast of total} & \text{Last year's total} & \text{This year's initial orders} \\
\text{initial orders} & = \text{initial orders} \quad \times & \dfrac{\text{from stores ordering to date}}{\text{Last year's initial orders}} \\
\text{this season} & \text{from all stores} & \text{from the same stores}
\end{array}
$$

A matched sample of stores is used in the calculation. Initial orders are also analyzed by four categories: this year's initial orders from those that bought the line last year; last year's initial orders from those that bought this year; this year's initial orders from those that didn't buy last year; and last year's initial orders from accounts that haven't bought this year.

Calculations are aided by punch cards having eighty columns covering twenty-two areas of information—one card for each account. This enables the forecaster to eliminate any accounts that are not a comparable match with last year's experience, such as an old account whose current orders are inconsistent with what they have bought in the past.

This method gives Jantzen indications early in the selling season of what's going on in the market, enabling them to make any necessary changes in marketing strategy and to adjust their factory production to match expected demand.

Initial-Order Forecasting in a Small Company

A simple, scaled-down variation on the Jantzen method is used by the Quaker Lace Company, a small (under $10-million) manufacturer selling to the garment industry and to retail outlets. Their principal problems in forecasting are the lack of reliable industry figures, fluctuating retail store budgets, and status of customer inventories.

They consult with their key account customers about three months in advance of the following six-month selling season and secure from them projections of usage by pattern and by month needed and feed this information into their computer. Sometimes this data also include individual stockkeeping unit requirements. Estimates are considered as orders unless confirmations are not received by a certain date.

Monthly revisions of the forecast are made to adjust to a rather volatile market. Simple forms are used showing the patterns and expected sales of each, with the comparative figures from the preceding forecast.

8i   To Assess Probabilities, Find the Standard Deviation

An offshoot of calculating the arithmetic mean, or average, to smooth your time series is figuring the standard deviation of each of your time periods from the average (or mean) of those periods. Then, by using a rather simple formula, you can determine the probability of a specific forecast figure being achieved.

Using the figures in the following example, suppose you wanted to determine the standard deviation of the five years from 1975 to 1979. You also want to know your chances of increasing sales to 450 in the period ahead.

	A	$A - M$	$(A - M)^2$
'75	325	-25	625
'76	300	-50	2500
'77	400	50	2500
'78	350	0	0
'79	375	25	625
	1750		6250

$M = 1750 \div 5 = 350$

$\dfrac{6250}{5} = 1250$ (average of the squares)

$D = \sqrt{1250} = 35.36$ (the standard deviation)

1. List the figures for the years in column A.
2. Add the figures in column A (total 1750).
3. Divide by the number of time periods (5). This gives you 350, the mean (M) or average of those periods.
4. Subtract this mean from the actual figures, as in column A − M.
5. Square these figures $(A - M)^2$, which eliminates minus values.
6. Total the squares (6250) and divide by the number of time periods (5), giving you 1250, the mean of the squares.
7. Take the square root of the mean of the squares to give you the standard deviation (D).

Now, having found your mean sales figure and the standard deviation from that figure, use the following table to assess your probabilities of selling more or less than the average. This is a standard table developed by statisticians. The first and last column are always the same. Only the middle column changes.

Probability Table

Standard Deviations from Mean	Values of A	Percent Chance of Exceeding A Values
M − 3D	243.92	99.87%
M − 2D	279.28	97.72%
M − 1D	314.64	84.13%
M	350.00	50.00%
M + 1D	385.36	15.87%
M + 2D	420.72	2.28%
M + 3D	456.08	.13%

What this means is that your chance of hitting the average—350—is 50–50. Your chance of achieving 243 is almost certain. But your probability of reaching 450 (or 456.08) is negligible—about one-tenth of 1 percent.

9

Improving Your
Time-Series Forecasting

9a Among the Methods Available and Their Characteristics

We have seen how the moving average of past sales (the time-series) can provide a pretty good basis for projecting sales in the period to come. But in short-term forecasting, which occupies most of the forecaster's time in most companies, seasonal, irregular, and calendar (and in many cases cyclical) variations take on great importance. These are the forces we've discussed before that make sales rise and fall from period to period, showing a series of peaks and valleys when represented on a graph.

In recent years, economists have developed a number of sophisticated methods to isolate and measure these forces. They give the forecasters certain mathematical equations to incorporate in their time-series breakdowns so that forecasting becomes more accurate and manageable, especially if many product lines are involved. Among these techniques are:

Census X-11 Method (formerly Census I and Census II)
FORAN System
Simple Exponential Smoothing
Double Exponential Smoothing
Winters' Exponential Smoothing

Box-Jenkins Analysis
Adaptive Smoothing (Adaptive Filtering)

These methods have the following characteristics:

They are mathematically more complex than other methods we've dis-
    cussed so far. Computer assistance is usually required.
They try to reproduce past sales results as closely as possible with
    formulas incorporating cyclical, seasonal, and irregular movements
    of the time-series.
They assume, as does all time-series forecasting, that the future trend
    of sales movement can be determined from its past behavior.
Most start with a moving average of past sales or some variation of
    such an average.
They have proved to be more reliable in short-term forecasting. In
    long-term forecasting, econometric techniques (correlating sales
    with out-of-company economic statistics) have usually proved to be
    better predictors of the turning points in sales.

On the following pages, we'll give you a condensed description of each
technique. More detailed information about them—with case histories—can
be found in some of the books and articles listed in our Bibliography.

9b   Census X-11 Method (originally Census II)

What it is: A widely-used computer program for seasonally adjusting a
time-series, using the ratio-to-moving-average method on a large-scale
basis.

For complete details: Write to the Bureau of the Census, U.S. Department of Commerce, for Technical Paper No. 15: "The X-11 Variant of the
Census II Seasonal Adjustment Program." Also: "X-11: Information for the
User." The computer program is available to the public for a moderate fee
(see also Section 14f).

How it works: Sales figures over recent years are analyzed and projected about as follows:

Raw sales data is fed into the computer, usually by month.
Moving averages are made in multiple-month segments (Bureau of the
    Census recommends 5-month segments).

Index figures are developed to indicate the percentage by which a given month's sales exceed or fall short of the average in its segment.

The seasonal index figures are applied to past sales figures to obtain a seasonally adjusted series.

A print-out is made of preliminary estimates of next year's sales based on seasonal indexes of the past.

Index figures are adjusted for any unusual fluctuation in demand that the forecaster expects for any month in the year ahead.

The Bureau of the Census says it is continually doing research to improve seasonal adjustment methods on two fronts:

1. To improve techniques for developing the ratio-to-moving-averages used to compute seasonal-factor and trend-cycle curves, the moving-average weights used to compute the ends of those curves, estimation of trading-day data from monthly data, and handling of extreme variations.
2. To improve the use of multiple regression techniques (breaking down past sales figures in several ways to better identify seasonal and trend-cycle components).

Going Back to Census I—an Exercise

Perhaps the best way for the novice to understand the basic elements of short-term forecasting and the Census II and X-11 methods is to do a paper-and-pencil exercise based on Census I, the manual system that preceded II and X-11. The procedure and the worksheet are taken from Robert L. McLaughlin's "Sales Forecasting Manual," which is used in the Control Data three-day forecasting seminars conducted by Mr. McLaughlin.*

Seasonal adjustment procedures are estimations. Therefore they cannot be exact. And, although the modern X-11 program is a highly sophisticated computer program, it may not be necessary. Simple estimates of seasonality can be calculated rather quickly if you have five years of monthly figures. (In all seasonal adjustment methods, no month can be missing. If one or more of the historical numbers *is* missing, you must estimate substitutes.) In the worksheet (see Figure 9.1), there is a pencil-and-paper version of Census Method I. Do not write on this since it is your master copy. Rather, go to an office copier and make as many copies as you think necessary. Then follow the steps below.

*From SALES FORECASTING MANUAL, 3rd Revised Edition, by Robert L. McLaughlin. Copyright © 1975 by Robert L. McLaughlin. Reprinted by permission.

A. Raw Data. Work in pencil. Take the last *complete* five years and write the actual monthly figures in the spaces. Write the years over at the extreme right.

B. 12-Month Moving Total (Uncentered). Add up the first 12 figures in Table A and write this total in the first box in Table B. Now drop January from this total and add in the second January. Write this number in the second box in Table B and continue this routine until all the Table B boxes are filled.

C. 12-Month Moving Average (Uncentered). Divide every figure in Table B by 12 and put the answers in Table C. (An alternate method is to multiply every figure in Table B by .0833—which takes 1/12th of each.)

D. 12-Month Moving Average (Centered). Unfortunately there is a problem in *centering* an even numbered moving average, so note that Tables B and C had to be shifted so that the first figures fitted between June and July of Table A. Now that we have developed a 12-month moving average, we can center it here in Table D. This is done simply by making a *two*-month moving average of the figures in Table C. At this point many might say "rather than go to all *that* trouble, why not just make a 13-month moving average and be done with it"? Absolutely not is the right answer. For instance, suppose the company was a department store with massive December seasonals every year. Any 13-month period that included two Decembers would then seriously bias the moving average.

E. Ratio: A÷D. Now divide every figure in Table A (except the first and last six) by the figures in Table D. Put the answers in Table E.

F. Seasonal Factors. At last we have estimated seasonal factors. They are derived simply by averaging each vertical column of Table E.

G. Seasonally Adjust Data. Divide each January figure in Table A by the January seasonal factor in Table F. Put the answers in Table G. Do the same for all the other months.

To illustrate how such an exercise might look when completed, Mr. McLaughlin provides a worksheet with the figures for New Private Housing Starts for the years 1968 to 1972 (Figure 9.2). Housing starts, he feels, is a good series for this purpose because: (1) it is very cyclical, (2) cyclically it leads the rest of the economy, making it a "leading" indicator, (3) it has a very pronounced seasonal pattern, and (4) it is one of the most important national markets touching a vast number of corporations.

Incidentally, housing starts figures are usually reported monthly in terms of annual rates. Mr. McLaughlin has reduced these to monthly figures.

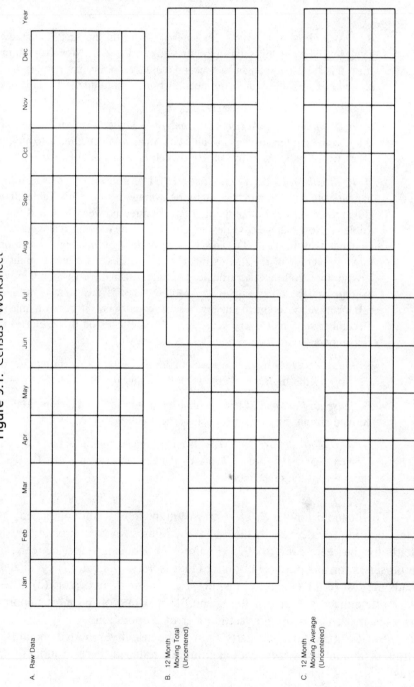

Figure 9.1. Census I Worksheet

A. Raw Data

B. 12 Month
Moving Total
(Uncentered)

C. 12 Month
Moving Average
(Uncentered)

D. 12 Month
   Moving
   Average
   (Centered)

E. Ratio A÷D

	Jan	Feb	Mar	Apr	May	Jun	Jul	Aug	Sep	Oct	Nov	Dec

F. Seasonal
   Factors

G. Seasonally
   Adjusted
   Data A÷F

Figure 9.2. New Private Housing Starts: 1968–1972

A. Raw Data

Year	Jan	Feb	Mar	Apr	May	Jun	Jul	Aug	Sep	Oct	Nov	Dec
68	80.5	84.6	106.6	102.0	140.9	137.9	139.8	136.6	134.3	140.8	127.1	96.4
69	101.5	90.1	131.9	159.0	155.5	147.3	135.2	124.9	129.3	123.4	94.6	84.1
70	66.4	74.3	114.7	128.4	125.0	136.2	140.8	128.7	130.9	140.9	126.9	101.4
71	110.6	102.2	167.9	201.1	198.5	193.8	194.3	204.5	173.8	179.7	173.7	152.1
72	149.1	150.2	203.9	211.6	225.8	223.1	206.5	228.6	203.0	216.5	185.7	150.5

B. 12 Month Moving Total (Uncentered)

Year	Jan	Feb	Mar	Apr	May	Jun	Jul	Aug	Sep	Oct	Nov	Dec
68						1507.5	1528.5	1534.0	1539.3	1536.3	1550.9	1560.3
69	1545.7	1534.0	1529.0	1511.6	1479.1	1466.8	1431.7	1415.9	1398.7	1368.1	1337.6	1325.5
70	1341.1	1344.9	1346.5	1364.0	1396.3	1455.6	1477.8	1505.7	1558.9	1631.6	1705.1	1765.7
71	1817.2	1893.0	1935.9	1974.7	2021.5	2052.2	2090.7	2140.7	2176.7	2187.2	2214.5	2243.8
72	2256.0	2280.1	2307.3	2346.1	2358.1	2356.5						

C. 12 Month Moving Average (Uncentered)

Year	Jan	Feb	Mar	Apr	May	Jun	Jul	Aug	Sep	Oct	Nov	Dec
68						125.6	127.4	127.8	128.3	128.0	129.2	130.0
69	128.8	127.8	127.4	126.0	123.3	122.2	119.3	118.0	116.6	114.0	111.5	110.5
70	111.8	112.1	112.2	113.7	116.4	121.3	123.2	125.5	129.9	136.0	142.1	147.0
71	151.4	157.8	161.3	164.6	168.5	171.0	174.2	178.4	181.4	182.3	184.5	187.0
72	188.0	190.0	192.4	195.5	196.5	196.4						

D. 12 Month Moving Average (Centered)

Jan	Feb	Mar	Apr	May	Jun	Jul	Aug	Sep	Oct	Nov	Dec
139.4	138.3	137.6	136.7	134.7	132.8	106.5	137.6	138.1	138.2	138.6	139.6
111.2	112.0	110.2	113.0	115.1	118.0	120.8	118.7	117.3	115.3	112.8	111.0
149.2	154.6	159.6	163.0	166.6	169.8	131.4	134.4	127.7	133.0	139.1	149.6
187.5	189.0	191.2	194.0	196.0	196.5	172.6	176.3	179.9	181.9	183.4	185.8

*E. Ratio: A÷D

Jan	Feb	Mar	Apr	May	Jun	Jul	Aug	Sep	Oct	Nov	Dec
78.4	70.2	103.4	125.5	124.7	120.0	110.5	107.1	104.8	109.8	98.8	74.4
59.7	66.3	102.2	113.6	108.6	114.6	103.6	105.2	110.2	107.0	83.9	75.8
74.1	66.1	105.2	123.6	119.1	114.1	116.0	103.5	102.9	106.9	91.2	84.0
79.5	80.5	106.6	109.1	115.2	113.5	112.6	116.0	96.6	98.8	94.7	81.9

*F. Seasonal Factors

Jan	Feb	Mar	Apr	May	Jun	Jul	Aug	Sep	Oct	Nov	Dec
72.9	70.8	104.4	118.0	116.9	115.6	110.7	108.0	103.6	105.4	92.2	79.0

G. Seasonally Adjusted Data: A÷F

	Jan	Feb	Mar	Apr	May	Jun	Jul	Aug	Sep	Oct	Nov	Dec
68	110.4	119.5	131.3	137.4	120.5	119.3	126.3	126.5	139.6	133.6	137.9	122.0
69	139.2	127.3	126.3	134.7	133.0	127.4	113.1	115.6	124.8	117.1	102.6	106.5
70	91.1	104.9	109.9	108.8	106.9	117.0	137.2	119.2	126.4	133.7	137.6	153.7
71	151.7	144.4	160.8	170.4	169.8	167.6	175.5	199.4	167.8	170.5	188.4	192.5
72	204.5	215.0	195.3	179.3	193.2	193.0	180.5	211.7	195.9	205.4	201.4	190.5

*These are percentages. In calculating, move decimal point two places to the left.

Chart courtesy of Robert F. McLaughlin

Mr. McLaughlin suggests that you count on taking at least two hours to complete this exercise, even with a desk calculator. To complete the housing starts illustration, with revisions to correct errors, took at least five hours.

These computations can be done in considerably less time using the Census II or X-11 computer methods. But doing this paper-and-pencil version is a good way to understand how a time series is seasonally adjusted.

Robert L. McLaughlin—"Mr. Sales Forecasting"

As we've said before, most sales forecasting concepts and formulas have been developed by statisticians and university professors like G. E. P. Box and G. M. Jenkins. One notable exception is Robert L. McLaughlin, developer of the FORAN method, whose background has been mostly in business and whose encyclopedic knowledge of forecasting should earn him the title of "Mr. Sales Forecasting."

Mr. McLaughlin was Marketing Research Manager for General Electric's Electronic Communications Department, then Director of Corporate Commercial Research at Scovill, Inc., where he learned the importance of translating technical statistical concepts and lingo into terms readily understood by the nontechnical executive. His boss at that time, Malcolm S. Baldridge—later U.S. Secretary of Commerce—insisted on having all statistical reports phrased in plain English.

Mr. McLaughlin carries on this policy of simplification in his present business, Micrometrics, Inc., where he publishes a monthly economic newsletter, "Turning Points," and a monthly sales forecasting newsletter, "Micrometrics." He conducts seminars on sales forecasting and serves as a consultant to an impressive list of companies. His three-day seminars on "Forecasting Techniques for Decision Making" are sponsored by Control Data Management Institute (6003 Executive Blvd., Rockville, MD 20852—phone 1-800-638-6590). They are held in various cities from coast to coast and can also be scheduled for individual company groups.

Mr. McLaughlin can be reached at Micrometrics, Inc., Box H, Cheshire, CT 06410, phone 203-272-3198.

9c   The FORAN System

What it is: A system of short-term forecasting developed by Robert L. McLaughlin, FORAN (for FORecast ANalysis) provides more flexibility and more features than the Census X-11 Method. It not only identifies the basic elements of the short-term series—cyclical, seasonal, and irregular— but also provides several possible forecasts, with guidelines to help in choosing the one apt to be most accurate.

FORAN has gained considerable popularity because it enables forecasters to choose the features they find most useful and economical. They can use the simple paper-and-pencil version (FORAN I, illustrated in Figure 9.3) for a limited number of products or, for larger-scale operations, the more elaborate computerized versions. Emphasis is placed on conferring with key executives before submitting the final forecast; with their intuitive feel for the market they can assess the possibility of such unusual events as strikes, machinery shut-downs, windfall orders, and so on—the irregular factors or exceptions that can throw the mathematically derived forecast off the beam.

Another feature of FORAN is a graph to help management visualize the percentage of change and the trend-cycle underlying the raw sales figures. Also there is a "forecast realization" feature so forecasters can determine their "batting averages."

For complete details: See *Short-Term Forecasting* by McLaughlin and Boyle: American Marketing Association (1968). It is said to be out of print. If unavailable in your library, it may be obtained from Mr. McLaughlin at Micrometrics, Inc., Box H, Cheshire, CT 06410 (203-272-3198). Also, a photocopy can be purchased from University Microfilms International, Ann Arbor, Michigan (313-761-4700).

How it works: Perhaps the best way to visualize the basics of the FORAN system is to follow a paper-and-pencil exercise. Here again Mr. McLaughlin has provided the worksheet, the graph, the example, and the instructions, which are adapted from his *Sales Forecasting Manual* by permission (Figures 9.3 and 9.4). Incidentally, this simple model has proved very effective in real-world forecasting, especially with relatively few important time series, such as major product lines. And it scored among the highest in the 1982 International Forecasting Competition sponsored by the *Journal of Forecasting,* in which twenty-four different models competed to forecast 1,001 time series.

Enter Seasonal and Calendar Factors

First, in Figure 9.3 calculate the seasonal factors for the next year,

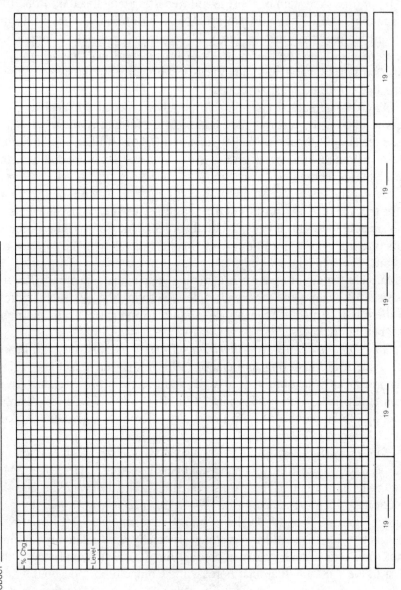

| | | HISTORICAL DATA | | | | | | MONTHLY FORECAST | | | | | 1st MONTH REALIZATION | | | |
| | | | | | | | | | | | | | | | % Realization | | |
MONTH	A Cycle % Chg	B Trend-Cycle	C Seasonally Adjusted	D Seasonal Factor	E Standard Month	F Trading Day Factor	G Original Data	H 1st Month Out	I 2nd Month Out	J 3rd Month Out	K Three Month Total	L NF 1 Original	M NF 1 Adjusted	N Actual Forecast	O Optimal Forecast	P R%
OCT.																
NOV.																
DEC.																
JAN.																
FEB.																
MAR.																
APR.																
MAY																
JUNE																
JULY																
AUG.																
SEPT.																
OCT.																
NOV.																
DEC.																
D%: ——— %	$\dfrac{B_{-2}}{B_{-3}}$	Moving Average MCD:	$\dfrac{E}{D}$		$\dfrac{G}{F}$						$H+I+J$	$\dfrac{G}{G_{-1}}$	$\dfrac{C}{C_{-1}}$	$\dfrac{G}{H}$	$\dfrac{C_{-1}}{B_{-1}}$	$\dfrac{M\text{-}N}{M\text{-}O}$

Figure 9.3. FORAN Graph and Worksheet

using Census Method II, X-11 Variant, or the simple paper-and-pencil method outlined in the previous section. (Most time-share and computer hardware companies have Census II, X-11 Variant, available for a small fee.) Enter these seasonal factors in column D. Also, if you use trading day factors (the number of trading or business days in each month) calculate these and enter in column F.

Enter Historical Data

As you receive the figure each month, enter the raw sales data in column G. Divide this figure by the calendar factor in column F (not used in this example) and put the answer in column E. Next divide the figure in column E (or the raw sales figure in column G if trading day factor is not used) and put the answer in column C. This is the raw sales data "seasonally adjusted." To smooth the irregularities out of these data, make a three (or five) month moving average of the figures in column C and put each answer (centered) in column B. (MCD at the bottom of column B stands for "Months for Cyclical Dominance," a statistical term meaning the number of months' span required for the cyclical component to dominate the irregular—in this case three months.) Next calculate the percent change in the column B trend-cycle data and put this rate of change in column A. The data are now ready for forecasting.

Graph the Three Basic Data

The graph (Figure 9.4) illustrates three columns of the historical data: (A) the rate of change is shown at the top, (B) the smoothed trend-cycle is the solid line, and (G) the raw or original data are plotted as the dotted line.

Make the Forecast

The forecasts are derived by multiplying the latest trend-cycle figure in column B by the seasonal factor for the month in column D. (Since we are using a three-month moving average for the trend-cycle, centering it means we lose the latest month.) Using the same trend-cycle figure for forecasting two or more months ahead assumes that there will be little or no change in this value—what's known as a *Naive Forecast* or *NF1*. In a time series with little change, this would provide reasonably accurate forecasts. But in a series with as much change as this one, the FORAN forecaster introduces a modifying value known as a "dampener." This is arrived at usually by experiment. You could assume that 50 percent of the change (as indicated by the difference between the latest seasonally adjusted figure in column C and the latest trend-cycle figure in column B) will continue in the next few months. So you use a 50 percent dampener. Another way to figure it is to subtract your MCD (number of months in the moving average) from 10 and multiply by 10 percent. In this case, the MCD of 3 indicates a fairly consistent irregular so you use 7 or 70 percent of the change as a dampener. To arrive at the best dampener, go back over your forecasts for the past year or two and see which one (anywhere from 1% to 99%) would have given you the lowest percent error.

Confer With Key Executives

Take your graph and forecasts to key executives who are most involved with the business and who might have special information or intuition about events in the months ahead that could affect sales.

Realization—Figuring Your "Batting Average"

To indicate your "batting average" on your forecasts, the chart provides several Realization columns at the right. In this example, it analyzes the forecasts for the first month out. The Realization columns are as follows:

L. *NF1 Original.* The percent change from the preceding month is calculated for the original raw accounting data in column G and reported in column L.

M. *NF1 Adjusted.* Do the same for column C figures.

N. *Actual Forecast.* Calculate the percent error using columns G and H (if it's for the first month out).

O. *Optimal Forecast.* Calculate the irregulars, using columns B and C—an estimate of the best we can forecast.

P. *R%.* Average the four columns above, without regard to plus or minus signs. Then calculate the percentage of change successfully predicted. In this example, 63 percent of the trend-cycle change was accounted for in advance—considered a good score. It's unusual to score better than 67 percent, according to Mr. McLaughlin.

9d Smoothing Techniques

In our discussion of working with a time-series to establish future patterns from past sales, we saw how seasonal and cyclical ups and downs could be ironed out into a trend line or curve by using moving averages. This is called smoothing.

Now, few companies or products have sales so stable that future sales

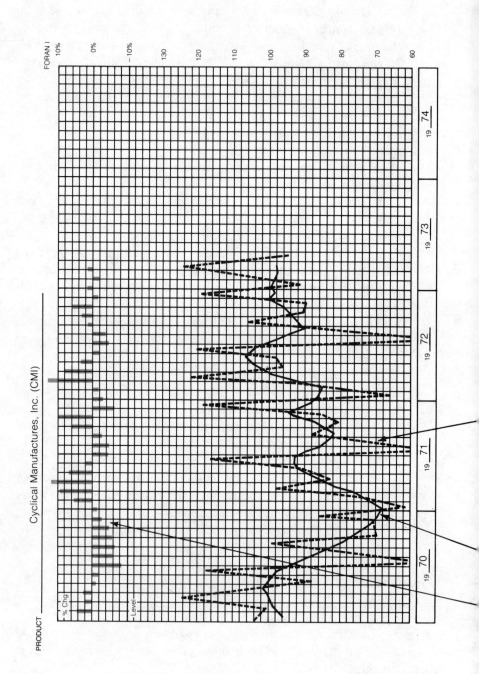

MONTH	A Cycle % Chg	B Trend-Cycle	C Seasonally Adjusted	D Seasonal Factor	E Standard Month	F Trading Day Factor	G Original Data	H 1st Month Out	I 2nd Month Out	J 3rd Month Out	K Three Month Total	L NF 1 Original	M NF 1 Adjusted	N Actual Forecast	O Optimal Forecast	P R%
			HISTORICAL DATA						MONTHLY FORECAST				1st MONTH REALIZATION % Realization			
OCT.	1.4	94.7	97.1	93.4			90.7	86.9	87.6	105.3		-14.7	5.2	4.4	2.5	
NOV.	4.5	99.0	94.7	94.5			89.5	90.3	109.5	93.2		-1.3	-2.5	-.9	-4.3	
DEC.	-.7	98.3	105.2	113.8			119.7	107.5	98.9	102.9		33.7	11.1	11.6	7.0	
JAN.	.9	99.2	95.0	96.5			91.7	92.6	94.4	95.2		-23.4	-9.7	-1.0	-4.2	
FEB.	-.2	97.0	97.4	104.1			101.4	97.2	98.9	98.0		10.6	2.5	4.3	.4	
MAR.	.9	97.9	98.7	126.6			125.0	120.9	93.4	91.5		23.3	1.3	3.4	.8	
APR.			97.5	98.8			96.3	97.3	96.4	109.6		-23.0	-1.2	-1.0		
MAY				97.5				94.8	107.2	54.2						
JUNE				110.5												
JULY				56.4												
AUG.				92.6												
SEPT.				116.2												
OCT.				93.4								18.6	4.8	3.8	3.2	63%
NOV.				94.5												
DEC.				113.8												
D%. __%__	$\frac{B_{-2}}{B_{-3}}$	Moving Average MCD: 3	$\frac{E}{D}$		$\frac{G}{F}$						H + I = J	$\frac{G}{G_{-1}}$	$\frac{C}{C_{-1}}$	$\frac{G}{H}$	$\frac{C_{-1}}{B_{-1}}$	$\frac{M-N}{M-O}$

Figure 9.4. Example of FORAN I Exercise

can be pinpointed by simply extending the trend line. Modifications usually have to be made to allow for past errors in forecasting and for seasonal and cyclical irregularities. This is done through the use of various smoothing techniques, some of which we outline herewith.

9e   Exponential Smoothing

What it is: Adjusting for past forecast errors can be done by a weighted moving average of past sales by periods, the average being modified or weighted in proportion to the error in forecasting the previous period's sales. This is known as *exponential smoothing*. Its purpose is to smooth out the errors of the recent past and enable the forecaster to adjust the current estimate of the average accordingly. In using this system, the most recent sales figures are given the most weight. Earlier ones have geometrically less influence. Exponential smoothing appears to be the most often used short-range forecasting procedure.

Special advantage: Ease of handling. If you're using, say, a three-month moving average to generate a forecast, you have to retain the three most recent sales figures at all times (and more, of course, if you're using a longer time segment). With exponential smoothing, all you need is the most recent sales figure and the corresponding exponentially smoothed average. This advantage becomes especially apparent to companies with a number of products or services, where the storage and processing of data needed to regularly compute simple moving averages would be quite burdensome. With exponential smoothing, most of these calculations can be done without computer assistance.

How it works: Select the time-period segment for your moving average that would give you the level of smoothing you want—three periods, four periods, five periods or more. Remember:

The more periods included, the better the smoothing effect.
The fewer the time periods included, the better you can track variations due to seasonal or cyclical changes or irregular factors.

Select your *weighting or smoothing constant* (also known as "alpha").

This can be any figure between .0 and 1.00.
In most cases, it will be between .1 and .5, and preferably no greater than .3.

Use this formula to help in selecting your constant:

Number of time periods
needed to produce an $=$ $\dfrac{2}{\text{constant}} - 1.00$
equivalent simple moving
average

Thus:

a constant of:	gives you the simple moving averages of these periods:
.1	19
.2	9
.3	5.7
.4	4
.5	3

This indicates, of course, that a constant of .1 would give you the same smoothing effect as a simple moving average of 19 periods, while a constant of .5 would be equal to a three-period moving average.

Since a larger smoothing constant gives weight to only the more recent sales figures, it will cause your forecasting formula to be quite sensitive to random variations in demand. This may not be desirable. To tell which is the best constant for you to use, you might do a series of trials on your past sales data, using several constant values, then select the one that best tracks your actual sales.

In our example that follows, we use a constant of .5 to reduce the historical sales data table. It would presumably be used only in the event of sharp ups and downs in sales due to irregular events. The forecasting experts suggest .3 as a happy medium.

Calculate the exponentially smoothed averages for each month (or other period) in your historical sales series, using this equation:

$$F_{(p + 1)} = C \times S_p + (1. - C) \times F_p$$

where:

F = forecast (exponentially smoothed)
p = most recent time period

p + 1 = forecast time period (one period ahead
of most recent)
S = actual sales (in most recent time period)
C = constant (usually represented with
Greek letter alpha in these equations)

Example: (Using a smoothing constant of .5 and assuming that the smoothed average for the first month is equal to the sales of the first month.)

Month or period	Actual sales	Smoothed average forecast
1	100	100
2	125	100
3	110	112.5
4	115	111.25
5	120	113.1

For instance, to get the exponentially smoothed average for period 4:

$$ESA_4 = \text{constant} \times \text{sales in period 3} + (1. - C) \times \text{ESA for period 3}$$
or
$$.5 \times 110 + .5 \times 112.5 =$$
$$55 + 56.25 = 111.25$$

Note that the exponentially smoothed average forecast for the fourth period (111.25) is comparable to the simple moving average for the first three periods, 111.66.

Don't hesitate to change your constant. Some people think that once they start with a certain constant, they have to stick with it through thick and thin. Not so. For instance, a manufacturer of household appliances found that using a constant of .1 (the equivalent of a 19-period simple moving average) gave him satisfactory forecasts, period after period, until a competitor came upon the scene with a product that was better quality and priced less. Sales started downward and forecasts were way off. Knowing that increasing the value of his constant would make his forecasts more sensitive to current radical sales variations, he changed his constant to .3, giving him the equivalent of a moving average of 5.7 (or six) periods rather than 19 periods.

9f   More Complex Smoothing Techniques

One possible drawback of the single exponential smoothing technique outlined above is that it doesn't reflect any linear trend movement in past sales data. The forecast formula we used assumes that the trend line of the moving averages (plotted on a graph) would be more or less horizontal. So the statisticians and economists have developed more complex formulas and techniques to reflect trends, cyclical, irregular, and seasonal elements.

We will briefly review some of them here. To be used properly, most of them require a knowledge of higher mathematics and computer skills. They are described in detail in such scholarly works as *Forecasting and Time Series Analysis* by Montgomery and Johnson, and *The Management of Sales Forecasting* by Eby and O'Neill (see Bibliography).

9g   Double Exponential Smoothing (More Smoothing)

To allow for the presence of trend in your sales history, you use the following series of equations, starting with the single exponential equation we used above:

$$F^{(1)}_{(p + 1)} = C \times S_p + (1. - C) \times F^{(1)}_p$$

Translated, this means: the single exponentially smoothed average for the period ahead (forecast period) equals your constant times sales for the current period plus the sum of the constant subtracted from 1. times the single exponentially smoothed average for the current period.

The single exponentially smoothed forecast you obtain from this is smoothed again to get the double exponentially smoothed forecast, using this formula:

$$F^{(2)}_{(p + 1)} = C \times F^{(1)}_p + (1. - C) \times F^{(2)}_{(p - 1)}$$

where:

$F^{(1)}$ = the single exponentially smoothed average
$F^{(2)}$ = the double exponentially smoothed average
p = the current period
$p + 1$ = forecast period (one period ahead)
$p - 1$ = period before current period
C = constant (usually shown as alpha—α)

Having your double exponentially smoothed average, you obtain your doubly smoothed current expected sales ($CES^{(2)}$) thus:

$$CES^{(2)} = 2 \times F_p^{(1)} - F_p^{(2)}$$

And the change in the exponential average (C) for the current time period thus:

$$C_p^{(2)} = \frac{C}{1. - C} \times F_p^{(1)} - F_p^{(2)}$$

Now you can compute your linear trend forecast for the next time period, using this equation:

$$LTF_{(p + 1)} = CES_p^{(2)} + C_p^{(2)}$$

9h   Brown's Exponential Model

Perhaps a better way to visualize the exponential smoothing process is to chart a simple series showing how the moving average and the average adjusted for trend are arrived at. The procedure was originally described by Robert G. Brown in *Statistical Forecasting for Inventory Control* (McGraw-Hill, 1959) and further elucidated by Robert L. McLaughlin in *Short-Term Forecasting* (American Marketing Association, 1968).

Referring to the chart, Figure 9.5 on page 95, proceed as follows:

1. Select your smoothing constant, alpha or α, in this case .2. Its complement is 1. $- \alpha$, or .8.
2. List raw data in column A.
3. Start by averaging the first three figures in column A and insert this in column D. (1000)
3. To continue this averaging, take .2 or 20% of the new figure (1200) and insert in column B; then take .8 or 80% of the preceding month's average (1000) and insert this (800) in column C.
4. Add columns B and C to get the new exponential average, 1040.

Smoothing Constant $\alpha = $ .2 $(1-\alpha) = $ .8 $\dfrac{(1-\alpha)}{\alpha} = $ 4.0

	A	B	C	D	E	F	G	H	I	J	K	L	M
		.2	.8			.2	.8				Forecasts		
Month	Raw Data	$\alpha(A)$	$(1-\alpha)(D_{-1})$	Exponential Average $B+C$	Change in Average $D-(D_{-1})$	$\alpha(E)$	$(1-\alpha)(H_{-1})$	Trend $F+G$	Trend Lag Corrector 4.0 (H)	Average Adjusted for Trend $D+I$	1st Mo. $J+K$	2nd Mo. $K+H$	3rd Mo. $L+H$
JAN	900								4.0				
FEB	1000												
MAR	1100		800	1000				50	200	1200	1256	1300	1350
APR	1200	240	800	1040	40	8	40	48	192	1232	1280	1328	1376
MAY													
JUN													
JUL													
AUG													
SEP													
OCT													
NOV													

Figure 9.5. Exponential Smoothing Model

Chart courtesy of Robert L. McLaughlin

To factor the trend into the average:

5. Figure the amount of change in the average (change from the preceding month) and enter in column E. (40)
6. Multiply this change (40) by the smoothing constant (.2) and enter in column F. (8)
7. To get the first trend average in column H (50), average the first *two* figures of the raw data in column A, then subtract this from the average of the first *three* raw figures in column A.
8. Multiply the first trend figure (50) by .8 and insert in column G. (40)
9. Add columns F and G to get the next trend (48) and insert in column H.
10. Having determined the trend in column H, you now multiply this by $1 - \alpha \div \alpha$ (in this example, $.8 \div .2 = 4$). So four times the trend, plus the moving average, gives you the average adjusted for trend. (Column J)
11. You can now make your forecasts, as indicated in columns K, L, and M, adding columns J and H for the first month, K and H for the second, and L and H for the third.

As each month's new raw figure becomes available, the forecast figures are adjusted accordingly.

9i   Winters' Method

Developed by P. R. Winters, this is a version of exponential smoothing to take into account both trend and seasonal movements in monthly and quarterly sales figures.

In this method, an independent smoothing constant is used for three components of the following general formula:

FORECAST
SALES   = the exponentially smoothed average adjusted over time,

          plus the trend factor as obtained in double exponential smoothing,

          multiplied by the seasonal factor for the period,

          added to the error or irregular component.

An independent smoothing constant is applied to each average, each trend and each seasonal component. The computer can be set up to select these constants automatically, or the forecaster can pick other values arbitrarily.

Mean Absolute Deviation—MAD (quicker way to
9j   measure the error)

In exponential smoothing, the error factor is known as the Mean Absolute Deviation. It is the sum of the absolute differences between forecasted sales and actual sales divided by the number of sales observations.

Using MAD instead of standard error calculations saves considerable time and paperwork. Standard error between actual and forecasted sales has to be determined, squared, summed, averaged, and the square root extracted. MAD will give you a figure equal to about 80 percent of the corresponding standard error, so multiplying MAD by 1.25 will provide an error figure that is about the same as the standard error.

Adaptive Smoothing (testing and adjusting
9k   for error)

This is also known as Adaptive Filtering. It is closely related to double exponential smoothing. It uses the most recent error to produce a new trend formula. It works best where historical sales data are available for a rather long span of time and past variations have been stable or consistent. Through a repetitive process, it derives the best weights or constants that will reduce error to a minimum.

Box-Jenkins Model (testing for trends, cycles,
9l   and seasonal variations)

This is a rather complex, computerized package. Its aim is to identify trends, seasonal and cyclical movements in the time series, leaving a series composed only of random, irregular movements.

To arrive at a model of systematic patterns in past sales figures, Box-Jenkins uses autoregression (AR) and moving averages (MA) to account for cyclical movements and differencing to account for seasonal variations and for trends. (Differencing is computing and tabulating the differences of a variable, in this case the time series.)

Autoregression is the process of determining a statistical relationship between figures of the same sales series in different time periods. Box-Jenkins autoregression is based on the assumption that sales in the forecast period are dependent on sales in prior periods.

The moving averages in Box-Jenkins are more concerned with past errors in forecasting than with the average of past sales. The average sum of past errors in forecasting sales is applied to adjust the sales series over time. In other words, how wrong you were in past forecasts has a bearing on how wrong you'll be in future forecasts.

The Box-Jenkins method assumes that the series is stationary, with no tendency for values to increase or decrease. If the sales series is not stationary, it is adjusted by using an ARIMA model (Auto-Regressive-Integrated-Moving-Average) which produces about the same result as simple exponential smoothing.

The Box-Jenkins forecaster experiments (by computer) with various mathematical models, using a repetitive process, to see which would have come closest to forecasting sales in the past. A more complex model, called a "multivariate," takes into account such variables as an increase (or decrease) in advertising support, special sales promotion campaigns, etc., which affect sales.

For periods not exceeding twelve months, Box-Jenkins forecasts have proved to be quite accurate. For longer periods, they usually fail to predict economic turning points. Also, considerable technical skill is needed to do the analyses and the extra computer cost and time involved might not justify the increase in accuracy that it might produce.

See these books for full details: G. E. P. Box and G. M. Jenkins, *Time Series Analysis, Forecasting, and Control*. San Francisco: Holden-Day, Inc., 1970; D. C. Montgomery and L. A. Johnson, *Forecasting and Time-Series Analysis*. New York: McGraw-Hill Book Co., 1976.

10

Forecasting with Econometrics

10a What is Econometrics?

Econometrics attempts to find and measure a relationship between your sales history and one or more "outside" series of statistics, or indicators, whose values are known and easier to forecast than your sales might be. It's a relatively new forecasting tool that has flourished with the growing availability of computer services.

According to our research study, this technique is used mostly by the large companies (22.6%), with medium-size companies (6.2%) and small companies (1.9%) trailing far behind.

Since sales in your business (and just about everyone else's) are tied to something going on in the economy, there's undoubtedly at least one set of statistics available that would show a reasonably close relationship with your past sales. Once this has been identified and tested, you assume that it will hold up for periods in the future.

For instance, RCA has found that they can anticipate the movement of their quarterly sales of color television sets to dealers by studying the quarterly movements of constant-dollar Gross National Product figures.

On the other hand, Branson Sonic Power Co. reports: "This method has been attempted with no success in finding a logical connection between variables and our sales."

10b How Do You Find a Good Indicator?

Look for one that is *logically related* to your company or industry sales, such as the industry forecasts put out by many trade associations. Beware of illogical indicators that seem to parallel your sales history, but could throw you way off the beam.

Try to determine the *reliability* of the indicator for at least five periods in the past.

Include a *broad-based measure* of economic activity, which will give you a clue to the trend of business in general, the likelihood of price and wage rate changes, and a feel for the general demand pattern as related to supply availability (for inventory strategy).

Look for a possible *lead-lag relationship*. Is there an indicator that leads the sales of your industry by a significant period of time? If so, try to define the lead or lag period. For instance, if your sales depend greatly on private home building, is there a correlation between housing start figures and your sales and, if so, what is the lead or lag period?

10c Some Economic Indicators and Sources

Survey of Current Business

Issued monthly by the Office of Business Economics, U.S. Department of Commerce. Each edition contains monthly, quarterly, and annual figures for hundreds of economic series, grouped under such broad headings as "General Business Indicators," "Domestic Trade," and "Construction and Real Estate," and industry headings such as "Textile Products," "Metals and Metal Manufacturers," and "Chemical and Allied Products." "Housing Starts," a favorite indicator for companies whose sales are influenced by the construction industry, is included in this survey.

Input-Output Tables

These tables show how sales in various industries are interrelated. Statistics and analyses are published from time to time by the Office of Business Economics of the U.S. Department of Commerce and in "Survey of Current Business" (above). This is divided into Transactions Table (dollar flows among sectors of the economy); Output Distribution Table (distribution of sales in dollars among all sectors of the economy); and Direct Requirements Table (amount of input needed to produce a dollar's output of any product in the table).

Drawback of Input-Output Tables: Since tables are developed from census data compiled every five years and much time is required to develop a full set of tables, there could be a lag of several years. But while some statistics might be dated, the relationships between various industries are usually stable. Large input-output models are maintained by academic and commercial organizations for use by individual companies, some of whom consider this the key to their whole forecasting effort. For a detailed description and two case histories, see The Conference Board's *Sales Forecasting,* pages 147–170. See also Leontif, Wassily, *Input-Output Economics* (New York: Oxford University Press).

Data from Your Trade Association
According to our study, this is the most popular source of out-of-company statistics, especially for small and medium-sized companies. (But about 10 percent complain that they have trouble getting figures for their industries.)

Data from Trade Publications
This is the next most popular source of industry-wide statistics. Many conduct yearly or quarterly surveys of the industries they serve and give frequent estimates of future business and trends. A good example of this is the *Cahners Early Warning Forecast,* described later on in this listing.

Help-Wanted Index
Described by *The New York Times* as "the index that's usually right," this analysis of help-wanted ads from the classified sections of newspapers was started by the Metropolitan Life Insurance Company back in the 1920s and is now maintained by The Conference Board. Since job advertising is one of the first stages in the hiring process, it is a good barometer of business intentions to expand or contract. A fall-off in job advertising several months in advance of the peak is typical as a recession approaches. Of the last five postwar business cycles (including the 1973–75 recession), turning points in the help-wanted index have preceded turns in the business cycle by a minimum of three months and a maximum of seven months—an unusually consistent lead time.

American Demographics
A monthly publication (started in January 1979) that keeps the reader up to date on demographic statistics and how to use them. Articles are informative, easy to read and well illustrated. Single issues $4, annually $30. Cumulative indexes available by subject, author and title, and books re-

viewed. Peter K. Francese, publisher, American Demographics, Inc., P.O. Box 68, Ithaca, NY 14850. Phone 607-273-6343.

Annual Survey of Buying Power
Issued each year by *Sales and Marketing Management Magazine,* 633 Third Ave., New York, NY 10017. Figures are given by state, county, and all cities with $10-million and more in retail sales. Most figures, except retail sales for most broad product categories, are given as both absolute and percentage of total and all information is updated each year. This is more useful to the sales forecaster than the Census of Population put out by the Bureau of the Census, which is published every ten years and provides no percentages of total figures. Retail sales figures (no percentages) are given for five broad product categories: food, general merchandise, furniture and appliances, automotive, and drugs. Information from this survey is available on data processing cards, which may be purchased from the publication.

Buying Power Index
This is Part II of *Sales & Marketing Management Magazine's* ''Annual Survey of Buying Power.'' It provides a weighted index by states, counties, and cities, with percentages of population, retail sales, and total estimated buying income.

Wharton School Econometric Model
This service is provided by the Wharton School of the University of Pennsylvania and may be subscribed to on a regular basis. It provides quarterly and annual forecasts for 61 series. (A special service at $2500 per year provides over 1,500 forecasted variables each month for eight to ten quarters ahead.)

County and City Data Book (for household data)
Issued periodically by the U.S. Department of Commerce. Household and retail sales data in nine product categories are given by Standard Metropolitan Statistical Areas. All figures are absolute, with no percentages of total provided.

Market Data Guides
Published by Standard Rate & Data Service, Skokie, Illinois. Gives estimates of population, spendable income, and retail sales in seven product categories for states, counties, and cities. No percentages.

Census of Retailing

Issued by the U.S. Government Printing Office. Census is taken every five years for years ending in 2 and 7. Volume I, "Retail Trade Summary Statistics," gives sales and number of retail establishments for 25 product groups by states, Standard Metropolitan Statistical Areas (SMSA), and areas outside of SMSA's. Volume II, "Retail Trade Area Statistics," gives sales data for 95 types of retail trade by state and SMSA. For counties and cities, data are given in 11 broad product classifications.

Statistical Abstract of the United States

Published annually by the U.S. Department of Commerce. Various economic series are given, mostly by states rather than counties or cities. Has a guide to other statistical publications and sources.

County Business Patterns (Employment Figures)

Published annually and available from the U.S. Government Printing Office. Shows number of employees for two-digit and four-digit Standard Industrial Code groups by state, county, and Standard Metropolitan Statistical Areas. No percentages.

Census of Manufacturers

Published by Bureau of the Census and based on survey of manufacturers taken every fifth year for years ending in 2 and 7. Volume II, "Area Statistics," gives total employment figures for all counties and cities with 10,000 and more population. Specific industry figures are given for states, counties, and SMSA's. No percentage figures are given.

Survey of Industrial Purchasing Power

Issued annually by *Sales & Marketing Management* Magazine, 633 Third Ave., New York, NY 10017. Gives state and county employment figures for all plants with at least 20 employees and large plants with over 100 employees—broken down by four-digit SIC industries. No percentage figures given.

Poors Register of Corporations, Directors, and Executives

Published annually by Standard & Poors Corporation, Skokie, Illinois. Similar to *Survey of Industrial Purchasing Power* (above) with data given by SIC classifications.

Monthly Labor Review
Issued every month by the Bureau of Labor Statistics, U.S. Department of Labor. Summarizes all major BLS bulletins. Has annual statistical supplement and articles on industrial relations, labor costs, price indexes, and current labor problems.

Business Conditions Digest
Published monthly by the Bureau of Economic Analysis of the Department of Commerce, this service tracks 300 economic indicators and is highly regarded by econometric forecasters, who call it the "do-it-yourself economist." Available at $40 per year from the Government Printing Office.

Business Cycle Developments
Published each month by the Bureau of the Census, U.S. Department of Commerce. Lists about 90 principal business indicators and over 300 components, relating them to leads and lags in the business cycle.

Federal Reserve Bulletin
Published monthly by the U.S. Federal Reserve Board. Gives useful data on industrial production, and monetary and credit statistics. Articles on inflation, recession, credit, prices, etc., give clues to pending monetary policies, which may influence sales trends.

Marketing Economics Institute
Publishes annual "Marketing Economics Guide," which brings U.S. Census data up to date; *Marketing Economics Key Plants—Guide to Industrial Purchasing Power,* a biennial reference work; the annual *Editor & Publisher Market Guide,* which projects data for every market two years ahead; and syndicated Target Market Studies. Address: Marketing Economics Institute, Ltd., 441 Lexington Avenue, New York, NY 10017—phone 212–MU 7–5090.

National Bureau of Economic Research
Has done a great deal of work in trying to identify series of data that "lead" or change their direction before the general economy and thus might predict changes well in advance. Has also developed "diffusion indexes," a

combination of many economic indicators to lower the chance of error. Address: 261 Madison Ave., New York, NY.

Cahners Early Warning Forecast

Published monthly by the Economics Department, Cahners Publishing Co., 221 Columbus Ave., Boston, MA 02116. Bulletins continually update and rate leading economic indicators. Their best leader is the *Cahners Early Warning Indicator,* which runs fifteen months ahead of GNP and most concurrent indexes.

Census of Mineral Industries

Issued every five years by the Bureau of the Census. Fifty mining categories are broken down at state and county levels for two- and three-digit SIC groups.

Construction Contract Awards

Estimates of the dollar value of construction contract awards for counties in most states can be obtained from the F. W. Dodge Division of McGraw-Hill Information Systems Co., 1221 Avenue of Americas, New York, NY 10016.

How to Use Correlation Analysis to Forecast with 10d Economic Indicators

Having selected an indicator that you feel would have a strong relationship with past sales of your company or industry, the next step is to test it and try to work out a "model" for forecasting.

This process is called *Correlation Analysis.* It is based on statistical regression methods, which for the forecaster means going back over a time series such as sales and calculating average values for past periods that can be expected to continue in the forecast period.

Regression models are based on comparison of company sales with the corresponding figures for an economic indicator, going back for at least five periods and preferably twelve or more if the data are available.

It's a good idea to start by plotting company sales and the correspond-

Tracking the Economy with Economic Indicators

High on the list of problems that beset the sales forecaster is the difficulty of gauging the state of the economy in the period ahead (see Section 3i).

To complicate matters further, economists and politicians sometimes come up with opposite conclusions based on the same indicators. For instance, in the hotly contested 1982 elections, Republicans called the unemployment rate a lagging indicator—even though it might get worse, the economy was really turning upward. On the other hand, Democrats were insisting that the worsening unemployment rate was leading a further slide in the economy. Past experience indicates that the Democrats were right. Before a recession and before a recovery of the economy, a worsening unemployment rate leads a worsening in the economy.

Knowing how economic indicators have behaved in the past gives you a pretty good idea of how reliable they would be in forecasting conditions in future markets. But remember that they are "indicators" and exceptions can and do occur.

Here is a list of some of the more common indicators and their average performance in leading, coinciding with, or lagging the economy over the post-World War II years:

Leading Indicators

Housing Starts—move up about five months before the economy.

Real Gross National Product—precedes the economy by about two months.

Stock Prices as reflected in the monthly Standard & Poors 500-Stock Index—leads the economy by four months.

ing economic indicator figures on graph paper, creating what's known as a *scatter diagram* (see example below). Then ask these questions:

How close is the "fit"? Using a moving average, can you show a general pattern to which a trend line could be fit?

Do the indicator figures lead yours, lag yours, or are they contemporary?

Retail Sales (deflated)—may lead the economy by a short period, but has usually proved to be coincident.

M-2 Deflated Money Supply—moves up four months before the economy does.

Coincident Indicators

Consumer Spending—has proved to be unreliable as a forecaster of an upward-moving economy.

Industrial Production—moves up as the economy does. Industrial Employment lags by a month.

Real GNP—leads by two months, but is generally considered coincident.

Deflated Personal Income—leads by about a month, but is also considered coincident.

Lagging Indicators

Prime Interest Rate—goes up 17 months after the economy. (Exception: its rise at the end of the 1980 recession, which contributed to a worsening of the economy.)

Unemployment—the rate goes down four months after the economy improves.

Investments in Plant and Equipment—improves three months after the economy.

A review of our economic history indicates that the more severe the recession, the quicker recovery comes in the early stages, but the longer it takes to get back to the levels existing before the recession.

Based on Leonard H. Lempert, "To Track the Path of the Economy You Need to Know Your Indicators," *Christian Science Monitor*, November 2, 1982.

How do estimates generated by the model compare with sales in past periods?

If the indicator doesn't provide an adequate explanation of sales in the past, select one or more additional indicators to use in combination (this is known as *Multiple Regression*). Throw out any indicators that prove wide of the mark.

An example: In their book, *The Management of Sales Forecasting*, Eby and O'Neill show how they constructed a regression model for a company producing an electrical component for big-ticket appliances. At the time, they thought that housing starts and durable goods expenditures would be two indicators logically related to company sales.

To test these two indicators, they constructed a scatter diagram for each one. A scatter diagram is one in which the vertical (y) axis measures sales and the horizontal (x) axis measures the economic indicator variables. For each period of time, a dot is placed where the values of the two axes intersect. Table 10.1 shows the data used by Eby and O'Neill in constructing their scatter diagram.

Table 10.1.   Data for Testing Simple Regression Relationships

Year	Company Unit Sales	Total Private Housing Starts[a]	Durable Goods Expenditures[b]
1963	248,980	1,354.3	53.4
1964	304,558	1,298.2	59.2
1965	291,727	1,472.9	66.0
1966	308,512	1,165.0	70.5
1967	356,190	1,291.6	72.6
1968	391,844	1,507.7	82.6
1969	475,486	1,466.8	90.0
1970	422,125	1,432.1	90.5
1971	425,690	2,052.2	103.5
1972	514,623	2,356.6	116.1
1973	567,639	2,045.5	130.3
1974	525,443	1,337.7	127.5

[a]In millions of units.
[b]In billions of dollars.

The diagram for housing starts (Figure 10.1) shows a hodgepodge of dots with no well-defined configuration, while that for durable goods expenditures (Figure 10.2) shows a linear trend that indicates a strong relationship between the two series. So housing starts was rejected and durable goods expenditures retained as an indicator for this company.

How to Measure the Degree of Relationship Between an Economic Indicator 10e and Company Sales

This is done with a mathematical formula to determine what is called the *Coefficient of Determination,* represented in most formulas as R^2 (R squared). R is the *Correlation Coefficient,* whose possible values, when determined by the formula below, extend from plus one (perfect positive correlation) to minus one (perfect negative or inverse correlation). A value of 0 means complete absence of any relationship between the variables. Square the Correlation Coefficient (multiply it by itself) and you get the Coefficient of Determination.

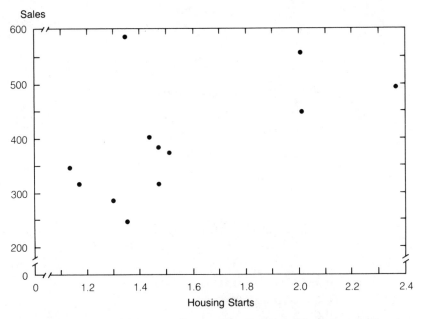

Figure 10.1. Scatter Diagram Shows Poor Relationship Between Housing Starts and Company Sales

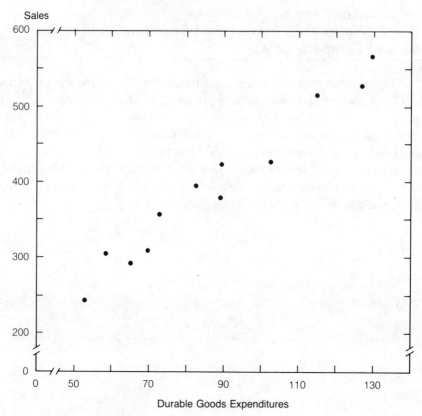

Figure 10.2. Scatter Diagram Shows Good Relationship Between Durable
Goods Expenditures and Company Sales

Here's the Eby-O'Neill formula for arriving at R:

$$R = \frac{N(\Sigma XY) - (\Sigma X)(\Sigma Y)}{\sqrt{[N(\Sigma X^2) - (\Sigma X)^2]} \times \sqrt{[N(\Sigma Y^2) - (\Sigma Y)^2]}}$$

N = number of time periods you are using
X = the Economic Indicator series
Y = the Actual Sales Figures
Σ = a mathematical symbol meaning "the sum of all,"
for instance, ΣX means sum of all figures in the
Economic Indicator series (in our example, this
would be 1062.2)

For example: using the 12-month data for sales and durable goods expenditures in Table 10.1, with all figures rounded two places for simplicity, square each year's durable goods expenditure figure and each year's sales figure. Then multiply each durable goods expenditure (X) by each sales figure (Y). Then total each set of figures, as shown in the table below.

Table 10.2.   Data for the Calculation of the Coefficient of Determination

Year	X	Y	X^2	Y^2	XY
1963	53.4	249.0	2,851.6	62,001.0	13,296.6
1964	59.2	304.6	3,504.6	92,781.2	18,032.3
1965	66.0	291.7	4,356.0	85,088.9	19,252.2
1966	70.5	308.5	4,970.2	95,172.2	21,749.2
1967	72.6	356.2	5,270.8	126,878.4	25,860.1
1968	82.6	391.8	6,822.8	153,507.2	32,362.7
1969	90.0	375.5	8,100.0	141,000.2	33,795.0
1970	90.5	422.1	8,190.2	178,168.4	38,200.0
1971	103.5	425.7	10,712.2	181,220.5	44,060.0
1972	116.1	514.6	13,479.2	264,813.2	59,745.1
1973	130.3	567.6	16,978.1	322,169.8	73,958.3
1974	127.5	525.4	16,256.2	276,045.2	66,988.5
Totals	1,062.2	4,732.7	101,491.9	1,978,846.2	447,300.0

Now, substitute the totals in the formula, thus:

$$R = \frac{12(447,300.0) - (1,062.2)(4,732.7)}{\sqrt{[12(101,491.9) - (1,062.2)^2]} \times \sqrt{[12(1,978,846.2) - (4,732.7)^2]}}$$

$$R = \frac{5,367,600 - 5,027,074}{\sqrt{(1,217,903 - 1,128,269)} \times \sqrt{(23,746,154 - 22,398,449)}}$$

$$R = \frac{340,526}{\sqrt{89,634} \times \sqrt{1,347,705}}$$

$$R = \frac{340,526}{299.4 \times 1,160.9}$$

$$R = \frac{340,526}{347,574}$$

$$R = 0.980$$

$$R^2 = 0.960$$

This R^2 (Coefficient of Determination) figure of .96 indicates that 96 percent of the variation in company sales over the 12-year period was mathematically explained by the economic indicator, durable goods expenditures. Eby and O'Neill believe that the Coefficient of Determination should be at least .90 to merit the use of an economic indicator in a forecasting model. (Forecaster Gordon J. Bolt considers any coefficient over .75 as a "highly reliable correlation.")

10f The t-Test

Is the Coefficient of Determination reliable or obtained simply by chance? To answer this, forecasters have developed what they call the t-Test or t-Statistic. Based on statistical theory and fairly easy to use, it indicates the chances of the coefficient being reliable, using a t-Distribution Table. A key element of this table is what's known as the *degree of freedom*. The rule is that for every constant you use in your table of data to compute the Coefficient of Determination, you lose one degree of freedom. In our previous example, we used two constants and we had twelve time periods. Subtracting two from twelve leaves ten degrees of freedom, which you would use as your key to the t-Table.

For more on this, with t-Tables, see:

Eby and O'Neill, *The Management of Sales Forecasting,* pages 114, 120–122, 154–155.
Bolt, *Marketing & Sales Forecasting: a Total Approach,* pages 194–195.

Publication information is found in the Bibliography.

10g Making the Forecast with Your Economic Indicator

So you've decided on an economic indicator that seems to have a good fit to your past sales figures. Next step is to forecast the period ahead, using this formula:

$$Y_t = a + bX_t$$

Tables, charts, and formulas in this section (10e) reproduced from THE MANAGEMENT OF SALES FORECASTING by Frank H. Eby, Jr., and William J. O'Neill, 1977. Reprinted by permission.

where:

Y_t = sales forecast at time t

X_t = the economic indicator forecast for time t

a = a constant calculated when the value of "a" is known, using the formulas below

b = the "regression coefficient" that measures the difference between sales and the economic indicator

First, you calculate the value of b, using this formula:

$$b = \frac{N\ (\Sigma XY) - (\Sigma X)(\Sigma Y)}{N(\Sigma X^2) - (\Sigma X)^2}$$

where:

N = number of time units used in forecast model

X = economic indicator

Y = company sales

Σ = "the sum total of all"

Having obtained from this the value of the b figure, you then use this formula to get the a value:

$$a = \frac{Y - b(\Sigma X)}{N}$$

Where do you get your X_t figure for the first equation? Many of the sources listed earlier in Section 10c, such as *Cahners Early Warning Forecasts* and the Wharton School, provide projections that can be used in sales forecasting.

10h More Complex Models and More Tests

We have just described a simple example of how an economic indicator can be found and used to forecast sales. In many companies, especially the large ones, the econometric forecasting models get quite complex, using several or more economic indicators. For instance, a steel company uses five indicators. Allstate Insurance Company uses 49! Some companies work a *dummy variable* into their forecasts to provide an alternate in the event of unusual or unpredictable events, such as severe weather, hedge buying in anticipation of strikes, or rumors of a competitive product coming on the market. This dummy variable usually has a zero value for all normal time periods and a value of one for abnormal time periods.

Then there's the test for what is known as *serial correlation* (or auto-correlation), where the difference between actual and estimated values for any one time period are not independent but correlated to the error for an earlier period. This test, whose computation and print-out are used in most computer regression programs for forecasting, provides the *Durbin-Watson Statistic*. It uses a formula that is "the sum of the squared first differences of the residuals divided by the sum of the residuals." A Table of Durbin-Watson Statistics is used to evaluate the resulting statistic, but values for fewer than fifteen time periods are not provided.

For more complete details, see:

Eby and O'Neill, *The Management of Sales Forecasting,* pages 155–158.

Montgomery and Johnson, *Forecasting and Time Series Analysis,* page 267.

Publication information is found in the Bibliography.

10i Other Methods of Developing an Econometric Model

There are a number of other methods to consider in developing an econometric model.

Share of Market

If you can get reliable figures for your industry, you can determine your historical share of market for each time period and see if there is a good correlation between the figures. If so, these industry forecasts can be used to determine what your share of market should be in the forecast periods.

In some industries, share for each firm is surprisingly steady (such as in rubber products, electrical machinery, professional and scientific instruments, and stone, clay, and glass products). Others vary considerably (such as apparel and lumber and wood products).

Points to consider in measuring the stability of shares (cited by Michael Gort in "Stability and Change in Market Shares," *Management Research Summary,* Small Business Administration, 1963):

Where several large firms are dominant in the industry, market shares tend to be more stable.

Where there are a variety of brands and brand names are important to buyers, there are fewer changes in shares in favor of either large or small firms.

Rapid changes in supply and demand contribute to share instability, especially in industries with a rapid growth rate.

Other factors influencing share of market:

Price-cutting
Shifts in distribution methods
Inventories in customer and end-user hands
New advertising and promotion plans
Increased number or improved quality of salespeople
Sales contests
Order backlogs
New products coming on the market
Style changes
More liberal credit terms
User demand
Mergers and acquisitions
Labor problems

Backcasting

This is a common method of *pretesting* a model to see how it would have forecast in past periods. Actual sales for some recent periods will be withheld and the forecaster will then attempt to "forecast" for these periods with sales figures and economic indicator values from previous periods.

Analysis by Markets

This is especially effective for companies with concentrated, easily identifiable markets, which are usually determined by *coding incoming orders by end use*. For instance, Bethlehem Steel uses American Iron and Steel Institute data on all steel-consuming industries to develop potential for each industry by basic market, by product, and by region. Its market shares of these sources in the past are applied to these figures to estimate its sales.

Analysis by Market Conditions

Especially in the larger companies, sales are affected by conditions in many separate markets. For instance, in forecasting appliance sales, General

Electric Company studies the conditions in retail outlets, the construction industry, and the second-hand market (whose growth affects the new appliance market).

Analysis by Distribution Channels
If you sell through several distribution channels—your own sales force, distributors, brokers, dealers, etc.—changes in any of these channels could affect future sales either negatively or positively.

Analysis by Territories
Where the sales force is set up on a regional basis, correlating company sales forecasts with regional statistics is reported quite effective. A chain of retail stores correlates its sales for each region with population and income figures for that region. Regional share figures are arrived at by dividing national figures by regional figures and comparing these with the chain's actual regional sales, enabling them to spot areas that are ahead or behind target estimates.

Analysis of Consumer Sentiment
A valuable tool for many companies in sharpening their econometric forecasts is the survey of consumer sentiment and buying intentions put out regularly by such organizations as The Conference Board and the Survey Research Center of the University of Michigan. The Conference Board reports that American Airlines, for one, makes direct use of these polls in its forecasting.

They have found a strong correlation between consumer expectations and air traffic, enabling them to forecast critical turning points and adjust company operations accordingly.

Rate-of-Change Analysis
See description and example of Cahners Publishing Company in Section 8e.

Company Example
Emery Worldwide

An Integrated Approach to Sales Forecasting

Emery Worldwide (formerly Emery Air Freight Corporation) is the pioneer of the comparatively young air freight industry. Its phenomenal growth has been due in large part to the advanced marketing and sales management techniques espoused by its chairman and chief executive officer, John C. Emery Jr. However, until recently, Emery did not have a sophisticated forecasting process. Its sales estimates were based largely on the judgment of its seasoned executives—still an important element in the Emery forecast.

Complicating the company's sales forecasting has been the recent entry into the field of a number of competitors, who are zeroing in on some of Emery's traditional markets. So it's vital to them to constantly monitor their markets and estimate the best sources of profitable business. To formalize this effort, Emery has set up its Planning and Analysis Department under the Vice President of The Planning Group. Forecasts are made for five years ahead and one year ahead, with quarterly updates. As for accuracy, their forecast for 1981, for instance, was off by only 3 percent.

Emery puts the most importance on these forecasting devices:

Sales of previous years. Because of rapidly changing conditions, only the two previous years are used.
Economic indicators and industry estimates.
Personal judgment of company executives.

Estimates by the sales force are given only secondary consideration, because of their inability to judge market prospects accurately, especially under highly volatile conditions.

Five Top Forecasting Problems

Here are the five things that give Emery sales forecasters the most trouble:

1. Lack of reliable industry figures.
2. The condition of the economy in the period ahead.
3. Actions by competitors.
4. How effective advertising and sales promotion will be.
5. Inability of salespeople and their managers to judge their markets accurately.

Emery's Approach to Sales Forecasting

At Emery, the approach to sales forecasting represents an integration of modern computerized statistical techniques, a continuing monitoring of forces in the external environment that affect the marketplace, study of historical trends, knowledge of internal corporate strategies that influence volume, and market research, coupled with senior management expertise and judgment (see Figure 10.3).

The External Environment

The Business Cycle has a major impact on the overall freight market. Accurate forecasting of industry growth relies heavily on an understanding of anticipated general economic trends as well as specific indicators which have his-

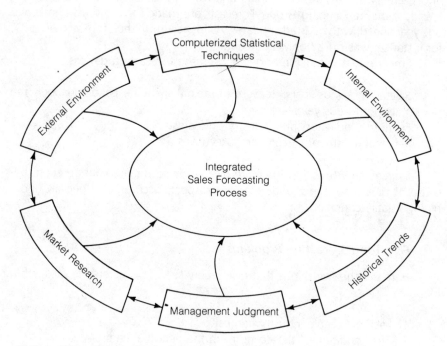

Figure 10.3. The Six Basic Elements of Emery Worldwide's Integrated Sales Forecasting Process

torically shown a high correlation with air freight market patterns. General economic indicators that provide inputs to the Emery sales forecast include:

GNP growth
rate of inflation
composite of leading indicators
consumer spending patterns
interest rates

In addition, industrial production indices, inventory ratios, and rates of growth of specific industries that have been heavy users of air freight in the past are continually monitored. Historical trends and quarterly forecasts for the key economic indicators are entered into the data base for statistical analysis and graphic display (see Figure 10.4). The economic forecasts are provided by an external consulting firm with which Emery has established a long-term working relationship.

In addition to the economic environment, another key external factor in sales forecasting is an understanding of competitive growth patterns and strategies. New entrants into the market, new product line offerings by existing competitors, pricing strategies, potential strike threats within the competitor organization or trucking industry, as well as historical competitive growth patterns are all closely monitored. These inputs contribute to Emery's estimates of competitive market share growth or decline, as well as aberrations in industry trends caused by strikes.

The Internal Environment

Emery forecasters find that open communications with all company departments is crucial to accurate sales estimates. Regular forecasting meetings are attended by representatives of Sales, Marketing, Planning, Finance, Pricing, and Operations. Management decisions on new product introductions, pricing strategies, market research studies, changes in the operational environment, impending internal strike threats as well as field sales inputs are integrated into the volume forecasting process.

Some of these inputs are scientifically analyzed. For instance, an internal strike threat in a specific city requires analysis of traffic inbound and outbound from that city, major customers whose overall volume may be affected, and an estimate of what competitors might try to capitalize on the strike in that city. Other internal inputs are not scientifically analyzed, but merely serve as additional inputs to improve management's judgment in the forecasting process.

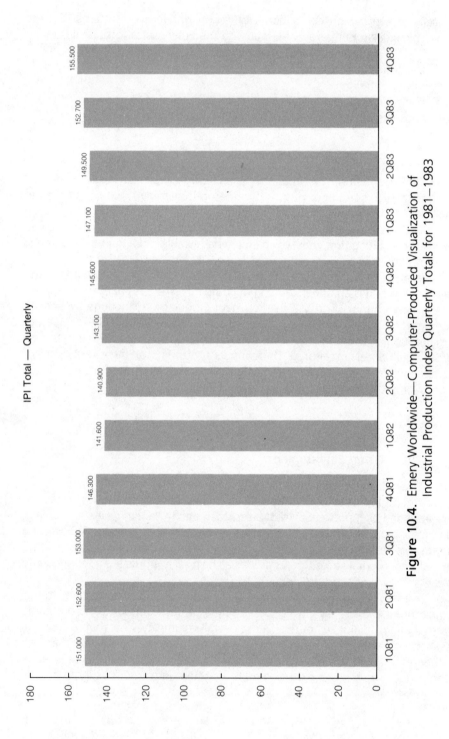

Figure 10.4. Emery Worldwide—Computer-Produced Visualization of Industrial Production Index Quarterly Totals for 1981–1983

The Role of Market Research

Regular studies are done in the marketplace on existing as well as potential Emery customers. Understanding the impact of advertising and promotional campaigns is essential to accurate forecasting of Emery's share of tomorrow's air freight market. In addition, the market research serves as the primary tool for new product line forecasting.

Past Is Key to the Future

At Emery Worldwide, great emphasis is placed on what they call their "historical data base." An important part of the statistical analysis portion of the forecasting process is observation of historical trends by product and how these trends have been influenced by changes in the internal and external environment. According to Shirley Lefkowitz, Manager of Business Control in the Planning and Analysis Department, this historical information is the key not only to future trends but to monitoring and assessing previous forecasting accuracy (see Figure 10.5).

A vital part of Emery's forecasting package is its detailed computerized record of every facet of their operations in recent years—by product line, by business classification, by customer, by region, by district, and by salesperson. This is carefully studied to spot cyclical activity, trends in customer usage, effect of competitive actions, impact on sales of advertising and promotional programs, etc.

Emery also studies the effect of business recessions of the past on their sales. The company averages the month-by-month figures of the past three recessions, how these were reflected in the Industrial Production Index, and how their sales volume fared in those months. They also try to determine from this information when business recovery is likely to occur.

Accurate Forecasting Vital

Accurate sales forecasts are vital to Emery's management planning and profits, says Robert H. Sykes, Director of Corporate Communications. With such a wide-ranging operation involving facilities, equipment, and personnel, wrong forecasts can affect service and be a drain on profitability. So the Emery Planning and Analysis Department uses every possible forecasting tool to achieve a high degree of accuracy in a volatile market. In addition to those described above, these include:

regression analysis
correlation techniques
identification of seasonality patterns

exponential smoothing
analysis of previous forecasting accuracy
graphic display capability, much of it computer-generated, to give added
   visual impact to the statistics.

The forecasting team is constantly working to develop and test new and
more accurate formulas for predicting Emery sales.

Management Intuition Important

"There is no scientific or statistical substitute for the years of experience
accumulated by our managers," Mr. Sykes points out. "This is an important
element to rounding out our integrated approach to sales forecasting."

Formal forecasting meetings are held twice a month. They are attended by
the middle line managers. The top brass stays away to encourage frank discus-
sions and minimize grandstanding. But the consensus of the group is reviewed
by top management, who contribute their own seasoned observations to the
process.

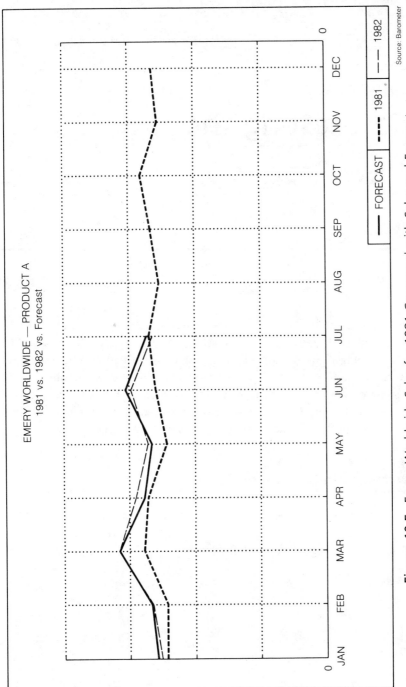

Figure 10.5. Emery Worldwide Sales for 1981 Compared with Sales and Forecast for First Six Months of 1982—Product A

11

Forecasting the New Product

Now we come to the area of forecasting that gives the most trouble—predicting sales of the new product. Here the stakes are higher and the chances of being right are considerably less than with an established item, what with limited information and experience. Because of the absence of hard facts, forecasters are apt to rely more on seat-of-the-pants judgments and "crystal ball" approaches. As a result, losses can be considerable, with an estimated one third of new products failing to make the grade.

11a Accuracy in New Product Forecasting

It's no surprise that accuracy of new product forecasting is less than that for existing products. Here's what the respondents to the Sales Executives Club forecasting survey reported:

	All	Small	Medium	Large
100% accuracy	0. %	0. %	0. %	0. %
90–99%	13.5	5.7	14.	20.8
80–89%	22.5	19.2	12.5	35.8
70–79%	20.1	15.3	23.4	21.7
60–69%	12.3	13.4	18.8	4.7
50–59%	12.4	13.4	12.5	11.3
Less than 50%	19.2	28.4	18.9	10.2

From these figures, it would appear that the larger companies have greater success with new product forecasting than the smaller companies. The obvious reason is that they have the resources to use the sophisticated and often expensive techniques available to measure market acceptance. And they have more experience in launching new products.

What Gives New Product Forecasters the Most
11b Trouble?

(Listed in order of number of mentions)

	All	Small	Medium	Large
Competitor coming in with similar product	34.6%	23. %	32.8%	48.1%
Judging size of market	31.3	34.6	32.8	26.4
Judging share of market	20.1	15.3	18.8	26.4
General state of economy	17.	17.3	14.	19.8
Lack of cooperation from dealers and others	9.	13.4	6.2	7.5
Judging initial investment	8.7	5.7	6.2	14.1
Status of customer inventories	7.3	5.7	7.8	8.5

With *fear of competition* heading the list of bogies, it's easy to understand why new product forecasting can be so difficult. It's almost impossible to canvass potential buyers of a new product without competition getting wind of it. This may explain why outside research organizations are not used more often in doing the market polling, as indicated in the following tally.

What Methods of New Product Forecasting
11c Are Used?

(Listed in order of number of mentions)

	All	Small	Medium	Large
We use our own research facilities	54.7%	40.3%	53.1%	70.8%
Our salespeople estimate the potential market	48.6	38.4	59.3	48.1
We use an outside research service	19.7	7.7	10.9	40.6
We ask distributors (or retail outlets) to estimate consumer response	13.1	19.2	10.9	9.4

	All	Small	Medium	Large
We figure rate at which item will be bought as substitute for another that serves similar needs and for which sales patterns are known	12.4	7.7	7.8	21.7
We do a study of purchase patterns after full-scale entry into market	10.8	7.7	7.8	17.
We study responses under simulated purchase conditions	6.7	5.7	3.1	11.3

Note: Two-thirds of the respondents checked more than one method.

Here are some comments:

In our industry a new product takes over a year to reach substantial sales and therefore we make no formal sales forecast in advance of putting it on the market. Budget estimates are kept on the conservative side. A new product is not sales forecasted until it is established in the market place. (Medium-size packaging materials firm)

Our product managers do the research on new products. (Large consumer goods sales agency; also medium-size industrial fabrics firm)

We market-test the new product in controlled areas. (Large consumer goods firm)

11d Some Questions for the New Product Forecaster

Is your product a *revised version* of an existing product, requiring no change in consumer usage habits, or a *really new product* requiring a change in those habits?
Your forecasts will contain more personal opinion or educated guesses as the new product becomes less related to existing lines and requires a change in buying habits. The less ''new'' a product is, the greater the opportunity to use objective methods used in forecasting existing products.

Is your management aware of the *risk* involved in forecasting new products?
If your forecasting for existing products is accurate, management may expect your new product forecasting to be equally accurate. Include a range of possibilities in your estimates to allow for the error that might normally be expected in this type of projection.

Point out the changes that could occur to alter your forecast.

Is your new product to sell in *concentrated* markets or *broad-based* markets?

Concentrated markets are easier to poll, especially in the industrial field where customers are easier to identify and reach. Sales department projections are apt to be more accurate in the industrial area than in the consumer goods field.

Are you launching the new product into a *growing* market or a *declining* market?

A growing market is much more receptive to new products and ideas.

Have you studied the *pricing* of your new product?

Unless your product is unique in its field, you have to price competitively if you want to get attention—and sales volume.

Have you provided for continuous *forecasting check-ups?*

Don't assume that what's true today will be true when the product is ready for release. A revised forecast can spot trend or economic changes as well as reveal new areas of sales opportunity and promotion.

Have you allowed a reasonable time *for commercialization* of your new product?

Many companies tell us that their estimates have been wide of the mark due to overoptimism about the time needed to properly introduce and commercialize the new product. With understandable enthusiasm about the new product and desire to get it on the market before competition gets busy, forecasters tend to be overoptimistic about the time required to prepare the market properly for a successful introduction.

Will you need to get into *partial production* of the new product to sample its acceptance?

Having actual samples of the new product to show prospective customers is usually the best way to get a good feel for its acceptance. How many units will be needed to "sample" your test markets?

11e Typical Steps in New Product Forecasting

These are, ideally, the steps followed by a company in forecasting new product sales. Many companies skip some of these steps to save expense or to get a product on the market faster for competitive or economic reasons.

1. *Estimate potential* for new product by historical analogy, substitution studies, Monte Carlo simulation techniques, etc.
2. *Probe prospective users* and "middlemen" to gauge their reactions. This can be done by using the sales force, and/or using company or outside research facilities to probe samples of the market.
3. *Go into limited production* of product based on findings in either or both of above steps.
4. *Do tests on actual use* of product to gauge user satisfaction and make any modifications that seem needed.
5. Do *late-stage testing* using carefully selected sample markets.
6. Keep constant *check on purchase patterns* once the product is launched full-scale on the market.

12

Some New Product
Forecasting Methods

12a Sales Force Estimates

What are the advantages of sales force estimates?

Since salespeople are *closest to the market*, they are apt to have a good
  feel for what will sell and what won't.
The company is apt to get a *broader base of opinion* than with sample
  polls.
Since the salespeople are already on the payroll and out there in the
  field, *research can be done quickly and inexpensively*.
Marked *differences in estimates* can give the forecaster clues to possible problem areas (or opportunity areas) to examine before presenting the final forecast.
With the salespeople directly involved in the forecasting process and,
  presumably, with the decision to go ahead, there's apt to be more
  enthusiasm and selling effort for the new product when it's
  launched.

What are the disadvantages of sales force estimates?

For consumer or nontechnical new products, the sales force *may lack knowledge* in many areas that determine consumer acceptance, so the estimate is more apt to be a guess.

Customers often reflect the optimism of salespeople and tend to give *overoptimistic responses.*

Salespeople may have a *bias against the new product* because of the extra time and effort they'd have to put in, so they might give a negative estimate.

Salespeople usually are *unable to detect general business trends* that could influence a new product's reception by the market.

Salespeople would tend to concentrate on getting reactions from existing customers and *neglect potential customers.*

12b User Surveys and Test Marketing

Should you do surveys and test marketing in-company or hire outside services?

Most companies say they do their own research, but more and more are using market research firms and consultants because of their expertise in selecting market samples and analyzing the results.

What sort of *accuracy* can you expect from test marketing under controlled conditions?

A grocery products firm reports accuracy within 20 percent.

Are user surveys and test marketing really more accurate than sales force estimates?

Yes, because of disadvantages of sales force estimating cited above. Also, you can gauge the patterns of repeat purchases, test various price strategies and promotional efforts.

12c Historical Analogy Method

Is there another product already on the market that is closely related to your new product and could be used for comparison?

At General Electric Company, the record of earlier similar products is reviewed to see how long it took each product to reach maximum sales. At CBS Records Division, new releases by an established artist are compared with sales of previous releases by the same artist, tempered by judgment concerning any changes in his or her popularity.

12d Substitution Method

Does your new product replace an existing one that serves similar needs and whose sales patterns are known?

If it's a truly innovative breakthrough, what is the probable rate at which users can be sold on making the shift?

12e Combining Estimates and Selecting Probabilities

Isn't it better to forecast sales of a new product in terms of probabilities rather than single-point values?

New product forecasters are increasingly coming to this conclusion. Since new product forecasts in the majority of firms are 20 to 30 percent off, it could suit your purposes better to determine a best estimate between optimistic and pessimistic.

How can estimates be combined to produce a reasonable forecast of demand?

A promising method is the Monte Carlo simulation, which is used successfully by Pfizer, Inc. Its basic elements are described herewith.*

12f B.O.P. and Monte Carlo at Pfizer

The challenge: To judge the best probability of return on investment of a new product, using computerized simulation techniques to rate the probabilities of outcomes of sales and other factors, ranging from optimistic to pessimistic.

The premise: Many variables have to be taken into consideration when calculating the success of a new product, such as:

potential growth in total market units
market price trends
price response of competitors
costs of new product
advertising and promotion support needed
general economic conditions

*Drawn from a presentation by Bradley W. Simmons, Director of Information Services & Planning, Pfizer, Inc., at the 1976 Marketing Conference of The Conference Board. Used by permission.

Forecasters draw upon whatever resources are available to estimate the reliability of each variable. For instance, the market for a new product to treat an ailment that occurs with known frequency in senior citizens might be forecast from Census Bureau data. Data for other variables might be drawn from experience with similar products in your firm or industry.

Pfizer forecasters define three levels of outcome for each variable being forecast: *Best (or most likely) estimate, Optimistic estimate, and Pessimistic estimate*—hence the B.O.P. acronym. Resorting to intuition, the forecaster might say: "I'd estimate that the market for our new product will grow at 10 percent a year. I'm confident that 95 percent of the time it will grow faster than 10 percent a year, and 95 percent of the time it will grow less than 15 percent a year."

One solution would be to combine all of the optimistic and pessimistic variables and then calculate a most likely outcome. But this could result in serious distortions due to overoptimism or overpessimism.

Looking at six variables, the likelihood that any four will simultaneously fall below a pessimistic cut-off of 95 percent is less than one time in 10,000 (.01%). Only once in 64-million times would one expect all six of the outcomes to fall within the pessimistic range.

Input Data for Monte Carlo Simulation

First-year key factors	Pessimistic	Best	Optimistic
Market size in units per year (000's)	7,000	10,000	15,000
Company share of market	20%	30%	40%
Fixed cost per year (000's)	$600	$500	$400
Variable cost per unit	$1.10	$1.00	$.75
Initial investment (000's)	$25,000	$22,000	$20,000

Based on These Assumptions:

Selling price per unit: $3.50
Market growth averages: 10% per year
Sales price, fixed cost, variable cost increases of 5% a year
Period-to-period market size correlation: 0.80
Period-to-period market share correlation: 0.75
Tax rate: 48%
Depreciation, straight line: 12 years

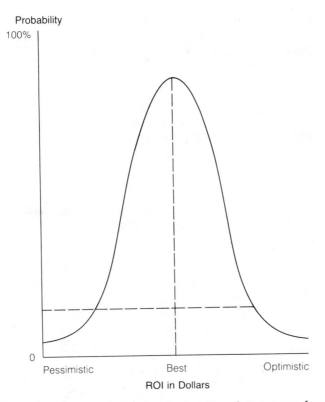

Figure 12.1. Graph Plotting Probability of Outcomes for Return on Investment

The Pfizer Solution—Monte Carlo Simulation

Pfizer calculates its B.O.P. levels for a new venture with a Monte Carlo simulation of their marketing world, feeding into the computer the logic they wish to use in their calculations. For instance:

$$\text{Estimated Dollar Sales} = \text{Price Charged} \times \text{Company Share of Market} \times \text{Total Number of Units Sold in Category}$$

The computer then randomly chooses from the range of prices, a price; from the range of market share, a share; from the range of unit sales, a unit sales figure. It multiplies the three, remembers the value of dollar sales thus calculated, and repeats the procedure as many times as it's told to.

Then the forecaster looks at the results to find out:

Has the data converged to some central value?

If, say, 200 simulations are performed, will the values be about the same as when done 10, 20 or 50 more times?

If looking at, say, tenth-year sales, has there been much *change* between the 150th and 200th simulations? If so, there could well be further change in another 50 computer runs, so it's repeated, say, another 100 times until a stable *average value* is reached.

To further satisfy the forecaster that the average values are reasonable, the levels of outcome versus the frequency of occurrence are graphed (see Figure 12.1, p. 133). If a convergence of simulations has been achieved, a familiar bell-shaped curve should appear, with the average value close to coinciding with the peak of the curve. The tails of the curve should fall off exponentially on both sides as one moves farther and farther away from the average value calculated.

Results of Running 100 Monte Carlo Simulations

	Lowest Value	Pessimistic (10%)	Most Likely	Optimistic (10%)	Highest Value
Sales revenue, tenth year (000's)	27,860	31,750	40,754	53,000	60,954
Net income, 10th year (000's)	9,393	10,429	13,833	18,167	20,644
Project present worth (000's)	9,197	12,778	20,809	29,375	40,659
Years to pay back	5.1	4.4	3.6	2.5	2.
Return on investment	22.9%	26.6%	34.3%	43.8%	62.1%

Satisfied that a stable average has been reached, the forecaster then commands the computer to come up with the Best, Optimistic, and Pessimistic outcomes expectable for the new product, from data used to construct the graph. It will give the *Best Case*, which is the most likely value it has calculated.

Also, a *cut-off level* for pessimistic and optimistic cases can be introduced. It might be decided that the pessimistic outcome is that level below which the project outcome might fall only 10 percent of the time and the optimistic outcome is that level of the project that would be exceeded only 10 percent of the time.

To determine the B.O.P. levels now, the computer is commanded to print out a table that gives the mean of the range, the expected value of cut-off for the high 10 percent, and the cut-off for the low 10 percent.

The forecaster now has a *realistic range of outcomes* and can be confident that 80 percent of the time the new product, if launched, will deliver results between those pessimistic and optimistic values.

13

Packaging and Presenting Your Forecast

13a Some Questions to Ask

So you've come up with a set of assumptions and statistics that you feel provides a good measure of what to expect in the period ahead. Your next step is as important as any you've taken so far—*to package and present your forecast properly*. As one respondent to our questionnaire put it: "Don't overlook packaging and presentation of the forecast—this can make it or break it." True, for if key company people don't fully understand it or see the significance of your assumptions and conclusions, the company (and you) may lose out on important opportunities.

Here are some questions you should ask about your forecast before you present it to top management:

Does it emphasize top management's chief concerns—profitability, volume, share of market, etc.?

Does it give the big picture or get bogged down in a mass of detail?
  Suggestion: Include any complex methodology and calculation details in an appendix to the forecast.

Do you use a standardized forecast format year after year?
  Advantages: (1) It can be prepared faster. (2) It makes comparisons with items in previous reports easier. (3) It assures coverage the

way the company brass like it. (4) It speeds comprehension of recipients familiar with what format to expect. (5) In a multidivision company, it assures that reports from all divisions will be uniform, with adherence to certain standards of conservatism.

Is your forecast understandable and usable by those down the line in the company, or do they regard it as only something for top management?

The forecast is a useful guide in line planning and day-to-day operation. Make sure that it's used or adapted to such use, so the company gets top mileage out of all your hard work.

Does your forecast avoid vague generalities?

Does it give specific expectations, including time?

Are charts and graphs used to better visualize major trends and expected results?

Suggestion: In an oral presentation, keep charts and graphs covered until you are ready to use and explain them.

Are major assumptions behind the forecast spelled out?

Assumptions such as expectations about degree of inflation, general monetary policies, tax revisions, general business forecast, industry forecast, consumer acceptance, pricing policies, competitive position of company, sales and promotional efforts contemplated or in the works. Where conditions are unsettled or unknown, alternate projections might be given for your assumptions.

Is comparable data included (from previous years, for company, industry, competition) for use as yardsticks?

Is the range of possible error emphasized?

As we pointed out before, no reasonable manager will expect 100 percent accuracy. The art of sales forecasting has not yet reached that long-sought goal. But it's getting there!

13b "Forecast Day" at XYZ Company

What routine do medium and large-size companies usually follow in preparing their forecasts? What follows is a composite picture we get from studying several companies that rely on monthly forecasts for decision-making. We'll call it the XYZ company.

The person usually responsible for carrying through the forecasting effort is the director of market research or market research manager. Every month a day is scheduled—Forecast Day—to get together with key company executives and discuss the forecasts. This is as close to the first of the month possible, after the accounting department has delivered the sales figures for the month. After these figures are processed by computer, the research director analyzes the print-outs and makes estimated forecasts for each product or product line.

At about 10:30 a.m. of Forecast Day, the forecaster meets with the sales manager (or each broad product line manager) and the production manager. Each person receives a copy of the preliminary forecast (they sometimes get this before the meeting) and each is asked if there should be any changes. In the discussion that follows, subjective information may come out that no objective forecasting method could anticipate, such as: "Our competitor has just come out with a product that's going to cut into our market by about 10 percent," or "We have a tentative okay on a big government order that will boost sales of that product by 15 percent," or "At the plant we're having trouble with the new packaging machine, so we have to shut it down for two days for repairs."

These are the unusual events that nearly every business experiences and that must be taken into account in planning. Meetings such as this bring out the "exceptions" and give those involved a feeling of participation and consensus. These meetings usually end at noon or before.

The forecaster then has a sandwich at his/her desk while revising the figures and developing a total sales forecast. At about 2 o'clock, he/she meets with the chief marketing executives—the vice-president of marketing, general sales manager, advertising manager, production manager, purchasing manager, and so on—to discuss the revised figures. Here again, information may come out that will require a further revision of the forecast.

Following this meeting, the forecaster gets together with the president or the general manager to get approval of the final forecast, which is then duplicated for distribution to the key company executives so they have it on their desks the following morning.

But no forecast should be considered as "final." Further unforeseen conditions are apt to come up. So the forecaster calls the key sales executives once a week to learn of other changes that might merit a revised forecast. And they are encouraged to call the forecaster as soon as they know of any such "exceptional circumstance" impending. This is all part of the "team spirit" that a smart forecaster can generate to make all company executives appreciate the importance of the forecasting effort. And thus are fused the two most important elements of good sales forecasting—the mathematical model and the experienced judgment of those who know or sense what no model can predict.

Drop Unnecessary Digits!

Your forecasts will be less cluttered and easier to understand if you use the least number of digits needed for precision and clarity in your numbers. For instance, 32,544,322 can be abbreviated to 32,544 or even 32.5 without undue loss of forecast accuracy.

The following table is used by statisticians as a guide to dropping unnecessary digits:

Table of Droppable Digits

When the figures in the series range between:			Drop
100	&	999	No Digits
1,000	&	9,999	No Digits
10,000	&	99,999	No Digits
100,000	&	999,999	Last 3 Digits
1,000,000	&	9,999,999	Last 3 Digits
10,000,000	&	99,999,999	Last 3 Digits
100,000,000	&	999,999,999	Last 6 Digits
1,000,000,000	&	9,999,999,999	Last 6 Digits
10,000,000,000	&	99,999,999,999	Last 6 Digits

Of course, you add to the top of each of your tables of figures, in parentheses, such advice as "Dollars in Millions," "Units in Thousands," or whatever your multiple happens to be.

14

Computer Tips for
Sales Forecasters

This chapter is for those who are not yet familiar with computers and how they are used in sales forecasting. You won't learn here how to select or use a computer—that would require another book. But we will direct you to sources of information and give you a few simple basics that may be of help to you.

Sooner or later, anyone who forecasts sales or uses sales forecasts in administrative work will find the computer an essential tool. For instance, the vast amount of arithmetic used in time-series analysis—especially in short-term forecasting—would be extremely burdensome and expensive without it. So it's important that the executive concerned with forecasting, as well as the aspiring professional forecaster, knows a few basic things about computers and how they fit into the forecasting process.

Before the arrival of the business computer in the 1950s, sales forecasting was largely based on executive judgment, aided by sales force estimates. Forecasting techniques used today, such as regression analysis and adaptive smoothing, were well known to statisticians. But for sales forecasters, the enormous number of calculations required did not justify the clerical expense involved. Most companies considered it cheaper to be less accurate and save the expense. The computer changed all that. All of the forecasting techniques can be used by any company with a computer or access to a computer service.

14a Overcoming "Computerphobia"

To the nontechnical person—and that includes most business executives—the computer is apt to cause an uncomfortable feeling at first. There is not only apprehension about being able to use it properly, but also a feeling that it threatens the user's years of experience and hard work, giving the advantage perhaps to younger, more adaptable people. To counteract this "computerphobia," most computer companies have simplified their instruction manuals and some give courses in computer operation. And a new industry of computer education has mushroomed in recent years, with courses being offered by hardware and software manufacturers, retailers, public and private schools, universities, and a variety of consultants. For instance, United Technologies of Hartford, Connecticut, recently hired a Santa Monica training firm to educate 1,100 senior managers and executives in how to use personal computers. According to a report in *The New York Times,* Dataquest, a high-technology research company in Cupertino, California, estimates that by 1986 the training industry will capture $3-billion of the $14-billion expected to be spent on personal computers.

14b Publications for the Computer User

Another recent phenomenon is the number of publications devoted to the computer. Most bookstores have special sections devoted to books on the subject, from elementary guides for the beginner to technical treatises for the expert. Also they sell instruction manuals for expanding the uses of individual computer systems, such as IBM, Apple, and Radio Shack, and software packages for many popular business functions.

Available too are numerous periodicals and directories on computers. Here is a representative list.

Periodicals

Business Computer Systems, published monthly by Cahners Publishing Co., 221 Columbus Ave., Boston, MA 02116. Emphasizes selection of new computer systems, computer peripherals, and business software. Features include product profiles and evaluations and software evaluations.

Business Computing, published monthly by Penn Well Publishing Co., 119

Russell St., Littleton, MA 01460. Devoted exclusively to business applications, problems and solutions. Features the "Top Ten" best-selling software packages.

Byte, published monthly by Byte Publications Division of McGraw-Hill, 70 Main St., Peterborough, NH 03458. Edited for the personal computer enthusiast, featuring instructions and technical information on building, buying, and using computers for private purposes.

Compute! published monthly by Compute! Publications, Inc., 505 Edwardia Drive, Greensboro, NC 27409. Devoted to the application of personal computers in home, educational, and other consumer settings.

Computer, published monthly by IEEE Computer Society, 10662 Los Vaqueros Circle, Los Alamitos, CA 90720. For the technically-minded. Covers circuit, component, and systems design, software programming and testing, and scientific applications of computers.

Computer & Software News, published weekly by Lebhar-Friedman, Inc., 425 Park Ave., New York, NY 10022. This is for marketers and retailers of personal computers.

Computer World, published weekly by CW Communications, Inc., 375 Cochituate Road, Box 880, Framingham, MA 01701. News about computer usage in various organizations, plus new products and services.

Creative Computing, published monthly by AHL Computing, Inc., division of Ziff-Davis Publishing Co., 39 East Hanover Ave., Morris Plains, NJ 07905. Gives in-depth evaluations of computers, peripherals, and software. Applications and programming techniques are provided for various levels of expertise.

Datamation, published monthly by Technical Publishing Division, Dun & Bradstreet Corp., 875 Third Ave., New York, NY 10022. Technical, semi-technical, and general articles and news stories on processing industry topics, with tutorials, surveys, "how-to's," etc.

Software Business Review, published six times a year by International Computer Programs, Inc., 9000 Keystone Crossing, P.O. Box 40946, Indianapolis, IN 46240. Articles on the use and management of computer software, showing how software systems can be used to improve business decision capabilities.

Mini-Micro Systems, published monthly by Cahners Publishing Co., 221 Columbus Ave., Boston, MA 02116. For sophisticated end-users structuring their own mini or microcomputer systems.

Online, published six times a year by Online, Inc., 11 Tannery Lane, Weston, CT 06883. For professional users of online database services.

PC Week, published weekly by Ziff-Davis Publishing Co., 381 Elliot St., Newton, MA. For IBM Personal Computer users.

PC World, published monthly by PC World Communications, Inc., 555 De Haro St., San Francisco, CA 94107. For users of personal computers, both technical and nontechnical. New hardware and software reviewed, user profiles, etc.

Personal Computing, published monthly by Hayden Publishing Co., 50 Essex St., Rochelle Park, NJ 07662. For people whose curiosity about the benefits of personal computer use is developing into serious interest and active involvement.

Personal Software Magazine, published monthly by Hayden Publishing Co., 50 Essex St., Rochelle Park, NJ 07662. News and reviews of selected software packages. Two or three buyers' guides in each issue enable comparisons of similar products.

Popular Computing, published monthly by Popular Computing division of McGraw-Hill, 70 Main St., Peterborough, NH 03458. For the professional consumer interested in using the computer for applications to business, home, and education.

Software News, published monthly by Sentry Database Publishing division of Technical Publishing Co. (Dun & Bradstreet Corp.), 5 Kane Industrial Drive, Hudson, MA 01749. For corporate managers and software professionals in business markets who use, recommend, evaluate, select, or buy software for mainframe, minicomputer, and personal computer applications.

Note: The periodicals listed above were in publication as of November 1983, according to Standard Rate & Data Service. This is not a complete list of periodicals in the computer field.

Directories

Apple II Blue Book, published semiannually by WIDL Video, 5245 West Diversey, Chicago, IL 60639. Software for Apple (and other compatible) computers from over 800 vendors, with ratings on overall quality, ease of use, vendor support, documentation, value for money, visual appeal, reliability, and error handling.

Computer Bookbase, published annually by McPheters, Wolfe & Jones, 16704 Marquardt Ave., Cerritos, CA 90701. A guide to computer science books with monthly updates and quarterly cross-referenced indexes. Has opinion columns and book reviews.

Computer World Buyer's Guide, published three times a year by CW Communications, Inc., 375 Cochituate Road, Framingham, MA 01761. Directories of computer-related vendors, their products and services. Listings divided into two sections: vendor profiles and product offerings.

Data Communications Buyer's Guide, published annually by McGraw-Hill Publications, 1221 Ave. of the Americas, New York, NY 10020. Products and their manufacturers, with addresses, sales office locations, etc.

Dataguide, published semiannually by Sentry Publishing Co. division of Technical Publishing Co., 5 Kane Industrial Drive, Hudson, MA 01749. Lists 4000 manufacturers and suppliers of data processing equipment and accessories, including software.

Datapro Directory of Microcomputer Software, published annually, with monthly updates, by Datapro Research Corp., 1805 Underwood Blvd., Delran, NJ 08075. 1200 software vendors and 2500 software descriptions.

Directory of Computer Software Applications: Minicomputers and Microcomputers. Published annually with monthly updates by National Technical Information Service, Commerce Department, 5285 Port Royal Road, Springfield, VA 22161.

Directory of Small Computers. Published annually with monthly updates, by Datapro Research Corp., 1805 Underwood Blvd., Delran, NJ 08075. Lists over 900 manufacturers and suppliers of small computers, software, peripheral equipment, periodicals, and services.

ICP Software Directory, Software Product & Service Edition. Published quarterly by International Computer Programs, Inc., 9000 Keystone Crossing, Indianapolis, IN 46240. Suppliers of data processing products and services.

International Microcomputer Software Directory, published quarterly by Imprint Software, 420 South Howes, Fort Collins, CO 80521. Describes over 5000 software programs offered by several hundred software publishers.

National Directory of Computing & Consulting Services, published annually, with updates, by Independent Computer Consultants Association, Box 27412, St. Louis, MO. Lists over 600 firms supplying data processing products and services.

Thomas' Register, published annually with updates, by Thomas Publishing Co., 1 Penn Plaza, New York, NY 10001. Has a section listing manufacturers of data processing equipment.

Note: This is a partial listing of directories available in the data processing field. For titles and descriptions of other directories in this area, consult *The Directory of Directories,* Gale Research Co., Penobscot Building, Detroit, MI 48226. It's available in most libraries.

14c A Look at the Small Computer Market (1983–1984)

Anyone who has followed the small computer market lately is aware of the numerous brands and accessories available, with more being offered every week and many formerly successful companies falling by the wayside. So anyone trying to select a small computer has a bewildering array of choices. Understanding a few basics of the market might be helpful.

First of all, a small computer is defined as anything between the big "mainframe" computer and the home device for playing games, making simple household calculations, and keeping records. The small computer field is divided into minicomputers and microcomputers. Minicomputers range in size from units not much different in functions from the smallest of the mainframes, down to the desk-top units found in many businesses. Microcomputers range in size from units not much different from the smallest mini, down to the hobbyist's home computer. With microcomputers offering more and more power and options at less cost, the dividing line between minis and micros is getting fuzzier and fuzzier and micros are replacing minis in most of the traditional functions. Because of this, the small computer currently is referred to as the Personal Computer.

Enter IBM

Apple Computer pioneered in the personal computer field, generating a host of powerful competitors such as Commodore, Radio Shack, Digital, NCR, Epson, Wang, and Texas Instruments (TI withdrew from the home computer market in 1983). When IBM Corporation, the undisputed giant in the big computer field, plunged into the personal computer market in 1981, it quickly took a dominant position despite premium prices and set standards around which the entire industry has gravitated. IBM departed from the usual industry policy of secrecy about operating details and published its technical specifications in order to encourage both hardware and software vendors to make products compatible with its machines. This compatibility and software support has been carried over to its home computer, the PCjr, introduced in late 1983 at a base price of $669, with 65,535 characters in main memory, ability to operate two software cartridges at a time, and a cordless keyboard that can be used up to twenty feet from the video display.

The versatility, compactness, and low cost of personal computers make it possible for each key executive of a company to have a unit right on the desk. The problem of getting direct access to data in the company's big computer without importuning the management information systems director has been solved with the development of software that standardizes the means of getting information from big computers to little ones. For instance, Data Resources, Inc., has developed a way for personal computers using VisiCalc to obtain detailed forecasting information from the main unit. Interactive Data Corp., Informatics General Corp., McCormick & Dodge, and Cullinet are some other firms that have developed PC software for accessing data stored on mainframes.

All this is a boon to the sales forecaster or the executive who wants to keep abreast of the latest forecast information. Forecasts can even be prepared or reviewed on the computer at home (using "MODEM" links to the office) or, thanks to the new portable units, on the road.

14d Elements of the Small Computer

To make good use of a computer, you don't have to know all of its technical ins and outs. But it does help to be familiar with the basic functioning parts of the typical small computer system.

There are six basic elements:

Processor	Keyboard
Memory	Display
Storage (disk or tape)	Printer

In most modern small computers, all except the printer (and sometimes the keyboard) are contained in one unit (see Figure 14.1).

Processor

This consists of two components: an arithmetic unit and a control unit. The arithmetic unit is the heart of the computer and does the actual processing with instructions from memory and storage relayed through the control unit. The control unit "reads" instructions fed into it, each instruction telling it where in memory to find the data that is to be processed and what is to be done with it. It finds the data, runs it through the arithmetic unit according

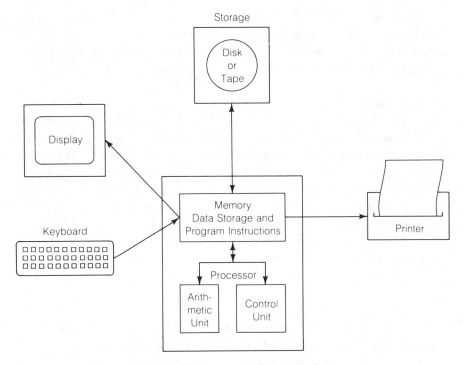

Figure 14.1. Basic Elements of the Small Computer

to instructions, then returns the data to memory, with the results of its labors being displayed on the screen or printed out.

Memory

When you get delivery of a computer, there are no data in memory. But there are instructions needed to get the device properly started and to allow you to enter additional instructions. These additional instructions are in the form of programs, which you work out yourself, buy, or have written for you by a programming specialist (see more on programs below). Every transfer of information requires a program instruction to move the data in the computer. Whenever you order a computer, you specify the amount of memory you need. Small computers for business vary widely in the amount of memory they can accommodate—anywhere from 64,000 characters (bytes) to over a million. Memory capacity has a great deal to do with the cost of a computer.

Storage

This is an extension of memory. Using fixed disks, removable disks, or tape, you can store data and special programs that you want to reuse. Most small computers now use flexible ("floppy") disks.

Keyboard

This is like an electric typewriter keyboard, but usually has a number of keys for special functions such as "scrolling" (moving the display on the screen when the characters or columns per line exceed the capacity of the screen). You type instructions to get the computer started and data called for by the programs you use. Manufacturers are trying to simplify computer operation by bypassing many keyboard functions with voice commands, light pens, and "mice." A computer mouse is a hand-held control for moving a cursor on the screen, which is a position indicator, usually a dot of light, that shows where you are on the video screen and where you want a character inserted or corrected.

Display

This is the TV-type screen on which the output of the computer is displayed. Provision can be made on most computers to illustrate data with charts and graphs.

Printer

This provides a permanent record of the computer's output. There are two types. The nonimpact printers use dot matrixes which are applied to specially treated paper by heat or electricity and can print as many as 225 characters per second. The impact printer uses either a matrix formed of thin wires or a "daisy wheel." Impact printers can make carbon copies, nonimpact printers only one. Charts and graphs can be produced on printers, using specially programmed instructions.

14e Some Basic Computer Terms Defined

To understand how the computer functions, and how to put it to best use, it helps to know some of the terms most commonly used.

Languages

Computer languages simplify the writing and use of programs. One word or abbreviation specifies a large number of computer instructions, saving time and laborious repetition. There are several languages or instruction codes used to program a computer to perform its tasks. Among those most commonly used are the following:

FORTRAN (FORmula TRANslator)   Used mostly in higher mathematics, science, and engineering where large numbers and complex calculations are required.

COBOL (Common Business Oriented Language)   A business language used by most large companies in their major applications programs.

PL/I (Programming Language/I)   Combines the features of FORTRAN and COBOL so that one language can be used in both business and technical applications.

PASCAL (Philips Automatic Sequence CALculator)   Easier to learn than the languages above, but has its limitations for business use.

BASIC (Beginner's All-purpose Symbolic Instruction Code)   A popular language with small computer users. Probably the easiest to use and can be learned in a few days, whereas FORTRAN and COBOL take several months' practice. Good for most business uses, but has limited capability for advanced applications.

ASSEMBLY   Allows programming in terms of actual program instructions rather than groups of instructions. Used mostly to tailor a program to a specific computer for performing a specific function. Fast and easy on storage, but hard to learn and read and is usable only on the computer for which it was written.

Efforts have been made to standardize languages, as programs created with a particular code for one machine may not work with another. But the industry is so subject to change and continual improvement that standards are difficult to arrive at and to maintain.

Bit

Short for Binary Digit, the smallest unit of information a computer can handle. Its value is either one or zero. Four bits are needed per digit and five bits for letters of the alphabet. Seven bits are used for capital letters and symbols. One bit is for checking and control.

Byte

Eight consecutive bits are called a byte. It's equivalent to one keyboard or print character, such as an "A" or a "7." Computer memories are rated in thousands of bytes, with the letter K standing for 1000, or kilobyte. For instance, a 64K computer would be able to handle 64,000 characters in its memory.

ROM

Stands for Read Only Memory. This is the part of the computer's memory that contains permanent instructions on how it is to perform its basic tasks. System software that is rarely changed by the user, such as "bootstrap" programs to get the computer started, program language translators, and basic data management instructions, is stored in ROM. ROMs can be replaced to change what a computer does, such as change character fonts on the display or the language used for programming.

RAM

RAM means Random Access Memory. This is the part of the computer's memory that is used by the applications programs to process and manipulate information. Additional RAMs can be bought to expand memory, up to the maximum allowed by the type of computer you have. Unlike ROM, when the computer's power is turned off, all the information on RAM is lost unless stored on a disk or tape.

Disks

These are either flexible ("floppy"), hard metal, or plastic disks for low-cost storage of information and programs. Disks have replaced tapes as the main storage medium for data. The disk drive and controller needed to use disks are either built into the computer or packaged separately.

MODEM

Short for MOdulator-DEModulator. A computer attachment for translating computer-generated information into audio signals that can be transmitted by telephone to distant computers or data banks. It also translates such signals back into electrical impulses that the computer can understand.

Software

This is the program needed to instruct the computer to perform specific tasks. Standard programs are available from computer stores, software producers (usually by mail), and equipment manufacturers. Custom-made programs for specific applications can be devised by in-company experts or by large software houses and programming consultants.

Hardware

This is the term used for the computers themselves and their mechanical accessories.

Batch and On-Line Processing

When data are recorded into a transaction file and processed in one run against the master file, the process is called batch. On-line processing is where data are entered in the keyboard and the master file is immediately updated. Often the two methods are combined, with input data being validated on-line but stored for a later batch run. Or revisions of records may be batched but inquiry to data in the master file may be on-line. Advantages of on-line processing: ease of validation and correction at time of entry; immediate access to current information; ability to display on the screen just the information needed in easily-read format. Advantages of batch processing: saving of operator time, especially when large amounts of data are to be entered; programs are simpler, requiring less equipment (all early computers could use only the batch mode); if power is lost during a run, program can be rerun from the start if recorded on disk or tape.

14f Questions About Your Computerized Sales Forecasting System

Assuming that your company has a computer and a knowledgeable person to supervise its operation, how do you use it to its best advantage as a sales forecasting tool? Perhaps the answers to these questions will give you some guidance.

What company series should be computed?

Sales billed is usually the series most companies use. If orders lead sales by more than a couple of weeks, this can serve as a "leading indicator" of sales. Among other operating statistics you might want to feed in are warehouse shipments, inventories, production rates, order backlogs, and prices.

What time frame should I use?

Most companies now forecast on a monthly basis. The computer enables you to maintain a continuous forecasting process, so you can plan for weekly, monthly, or quarterly forecasts, depending on the nature of your business.

What about programs?

Unless you use the right computer programs, your sales forecasting effort will be inaccurate, burdensome, and expensive. Here the well-known rule of the computer trade applies—GIGO: Garbage In, Garbage Out. Large companies with big computer systems have professional staffs that write the programs they need. Smaller users rely on packaged applications programs or on professional programming consultants. These programs, which usually come on disk or tape with instructions, are available from systems houses who design the entire computer installation from hardware to customized programs, computer stores, some bookstores, software houses, and equipment manufacturers. No manufacturer, including giant IBM, can provide the vast amount of programming required. So they leave much of this development to software firms. There are hundreds of these, ranging in size from one-man operations to huge establishments with hundreds of programmers. These software houses sell to users by mail order, through computer stores, and original equipment manufacturers. Most of the manufacturers have a catalogue of software programs that work well with their equipment. For instance, Apple Computer, Inc., publishes an annual directory of programs available from over 800 companies, with ratings on their overall quality, ease of use, vendor support, documentation, value for the money, visual appeal, reliability, and error handling.

What should a beginner look for in software programs?

If you're a beginner in computer use, you should look for a program that is "user-oriented," or geared to the neophyte. Packages that are easiest to learn and implement are described as "menu-driven." The "menu" lists all choices open to the operator and gives simple instructions on how to execute the desired choices. There are also "sub-menus" with more detailed instructions. Try to get a demonstration of a software program before you buy it. And find out whom you can call to answer any questions you have.

Here are some questions you should answer about a piece of software to be sure you can use it with your equipment:

1. Do you need a specific operating system or version of the system? For instance, the CP/M system of Digital Research, Inc., which operates on 8-bit machines, won't work on IBM's 16-bit equipment. IBM's operating system, called MS-DOS (designed by Microsoft), appears at this writing to be the best bet to become the industry standard.
2. Is your computer's memory adequate to handle the software program? If not, can you add more memory to your computer, or choose another program requiring less memory?
3. How about your computer storage? Some software packages require

Winchester or hard disk storage, others floppy disk only. Are two drives needed instead of one?

4. Does the package specify a particular language or level of the language?
5. Is a printer required? If so, must it be a specific brand? How many columns wide?
6. Are special function keys needed?

What are some of the software programs for sales forecasting?

Programs are available for most sales forecasting methods, from simple regression to least-squares curve fitting. There seems to be no central source of such programs. You have to dig them out of catalogues, computer publications, and economics journals. Here are a few of them to show the range of what was available in 1983. Prices given are for comparison and are subject to change.

VisiCalc

This is a good (and very popular) program for most computer systems, providing powerful planning and forecasting functions. The display screen becomes an electronic worksheet ("spreadsheet") of columns and rows. You decide on the formulas you will use, enter the figures, and VisiCalc will do whatever calculations and manipulations of figures you want. When any position's value changes, all other items dependent on that value change automatically. It's especially good for reviewing a "what if?" situation in seconds. When projecting annual sales, for instance, you might want to know what would happen if September sales increased by 7.5 percent. The VisiCalc software would instantly recalculate the ensuing months' sales projections, using a constant or variable exponents. Your electronic worksheet can be saved on disk for later use, or printed out. Available from VisiCorp., 2895 Zanker Blvd., San Jose, CA 95131. Requires a minimum of 48K memory. Disk, four-lesson instructions with illustrations and 144-page command reference guide. Assembly language. Price $250. (Other companies such as Radio Shack are licensed to sell VisiCalc.) A new VisiCorp program, Visi-On, combines the spreadsheet with word processing and graphing functions.

Lotus 1–2–3

This was the leader in wrapping several successful programs into an integrated package. It combines a spreadsheet (similar to VisiCalc) with graphics and a database manager. It operates on the IBM Personal Computer and all IBM-compatible machines. Produced by Lotus Development Corp., Cambridge, Massachusetts (price about $500). Among similar spreadsheet packages are Visi-On, mentioned above, Contex MBA, and Multiplan.

Do-it-Yourself Programs

A book, "Basic Computer Programs for Business," by Charles D. Sternberg, gives coding instructions for three forecasting methods—least squares regression forecasting, moving average forecasting, and exponential smoothing forecasting. (Other business applications programs are also included.) Published by Hayden Book Co., Rochelle Park, NJ. Available at most bookstores. Price $10.95.

Census II, X-11

The eleventh version of Census Method II (see Section 9b) is the standard for forecasters all over the world. It seasonally adjusts the time-series and forecasts the seasonal pattern, but does not forecast sales. The forecaster does this with the aid of output tables provided for guidance. X-11 can also analyze the company series in relation to economic indicators and national business cycles. This program is available from the Census Bureau of the Department of Commerce for a nominal fee (about $100). For details, write or call Mort Somer (301-763-5768).

FORAN III

This program piggybacks on Census X-11, but is specifically oriented to sales forecasting in business organizations (see Section 9c). The simpler model, FORAN I, can easily be programmed in BASIC or VisiCalc. FORAN III is an improved version of the two earlier models. For further information: Micrometrics, Inc., Box H, Cheshire, CT 06410 (203-272-3198).

How can I be sure that I have the best computerized sales forecasting program?

For the computer novice—and even for someone familiar with computer usage—searching for the right sales forecasting programs and adapting them to your hardware and to your company's needs can be a rather frustrating, time-consuming experience. And every week, it seems, new programs or new versions of existing programs are offered. What should you do to assure that you have a system that will do your forecasting with a minimum of effort and error? An obvious source of help would be the systems house, equipment manufacturer, or dealer who sold you your computer hardware. But neither large nor small vendors can afford to customize programs for each buyer.

For many companies—large, medium, and small—the answer may be the independent computer programming consultant. Usually, the small or medium company will balk at the idea of calling in such a consultant, fearing that the rates will be too high. Yet they don't hesitate to hire a CPA, a lawyer, or other professionals to contribute expertise to other facets of company operation.

Do I need a generalist or a programmer?

There are two types of computer consultants—the generalists and the programmers. The generalist works with the whole system from selection of hardware to programming. The programmer specializes in selecting, adapting, and debugging the software programs that will make your system run smoothly. Generalists do programming too, but programmers are apt to be better for specific, detailed applications such as sales forecasting.

How can I find a good programmer?

A programming specialist must be thoroughly familiar with forecasting techniques, with your equipment, and with the program language you're using. Perhaps the best source of such consultants is the firm that sold you your computer equipment. They usually maintain a list of reliable consultants who are proficient in using their products and whose expertise they believe will assure more satisfied customers.

How much do programmers cost and how can I cut costs?

Computer programmer fees range between $200 and $500 a day. You can reduce the overall cost in several ways:

Before you interview the programmer, prepare an outline of the forecasting techniques you wish to use, the number or products or product lines you have, the frequency of forecasts desired, etc. In the interview, get an estimate of the time required to set up your system and any off-the-shelf packaged programs that might be used or adapted.

Before the programmer starts work, compile all of the statistics that will be needed—sales history, seasonal characteristics, etc. Don't make the programmer have to dig it out. You'll pay for it.

Find out what other information will be needed. Some programmers provide their own data-gathering forms.

Will you want to use graphics—computer-generated charts and graphs? This facility is available on most computer systems at reasonable cost and greatly enhances the visual impact of your forecasts.

Don't hesitate to hire the consultant for only one or two days. Maybe all you need is help in getting properly started, or suggestions for improving a program you already have.

If you won't be working with the programmer yourself, assign a staff member thoroughly knowledgeable about your business to be the liaison, providing any missing data and answering questions on the spot.

Should I use a time-shared computer?

Any forecaster who has an occasionally large and tedious number of calculations to make should look into the advisability of using the time-shared computer company. There are many of these and most have good programs for developing multiple regression equations. They are especially useful if you want to test a number of independent variables and don't want to tie up the office machine. But learning how to run a time-shared computer isn't easy. You must learn how to enter the instructions on your computer keyboard for the distant computer to follow, using a basic language code. When you have signaled the time-shared computer what you wish to have done, it flashes on your screen a series of questions for you to answer and indicates the data needed. Among the time-shared computer firms widely used and recommended by sales forecasters are Rapidata, Inc., Fairfield, NJ, and Control Data Corp., Rockville, MD. These and other such firms have branch facilities in many of the larger cities.

15

A Forecaster's Abridged Dictionary

Here are definitions of some terms frequently encountered in sales forecasting literature. References in parentheses refer to sections of this report where the term is defined further. A review of these terms will give the reader further insight into the scope and increasing sophistication of the sales forecasting process.

Adaptive filtering—Much the same as exponential smoothing. Through a repetitive process, it derives the optimum weights to apply to the forecast to reduce the error to a minimum. (9k)

Alpha—A weighting constant in smoothing equations that determines the proportional rate at which a forecast responds to the most recent sales observation. (9e)

ARIMA models—Auto-Regressive Integrated Moving Average formulas used in Box-Jenkins forecasting to calculate the effect of trends and cyclical and seasonal movements on past sales in order to predict their influence on forecasted sales. (9l)

Arithmetic paper—Graph paper ruled to conform to regular arithmetical values. See also *Log paper*.

Autocorrelation—A measure of the degree of association of any pair of observations that are a certain number of periods apart. Also called *Serial Correlation*. (10h)

Autoregression—Determining the statistical relationship between a current observation and a previous finding in the same time series. (9l)

Average—The sum of all the numbers divided by the number of numbers. (8c)

Averaging method—Combining two or more forecast series by averaging them together.

Bayesian Analysis—Essentially a method of using judgment or hunches to assign probabilities to the outcomes of various courses of action and then, based on results of traditional test marketing, selecting the most promising forecast.

Bench mark—The basic sales figure or other data from which subsequent figures are derived through sampling.

"Black box" model—A concept presented by P. Kotler in the *Journal of Marketing* (October 1965) comparing the buyer's psyche to a "black box" whose workings can be figured out only partially. A behavioral model seeks to explain what happens between the input and the output of the "black box."

"Black-box Syndrome"—The skepticism some managements have about seemingly exotic forecasting techniques that they do not clearly understand.

Bottom-up approach—Using the reports from the sales force and customers as the basis for forecasting. Regarded as reliable only in short-term forecasting. See *Top-down Approach*.

Box-Jenkins Model—A computerized method of selecting the specific time series formula which over past periods would have produced the most accurate forecasts. It attempts to account for trend, seasonal, and cyclical movements, leaving a series made up of only random, irregular movements. It relies on autoregression and moving averages to account for cyclical movements and upon differencing to account for seasonal and secular movements. (9l)

Business cycle—See *Cycles*.

Causality—A cause-and-effect relationship.

Causal Model—A forecasting model that shows an influencing relationship between the time series of interest and one or more other time series. If these other series seem to correlate with the series of interest and there seems to be some cause for this correlation, a statistical model can be constructed showing this relationship.

Census II Method (Also Census X-11 Method)—A computerized technique developed by the Census Bureau for seasonally adjusting a time series (ironing out the seasonal variations), making the application of the ratio-to-moving-average method possible on a large scale. (9b)

Census tract—Data on a section of a city or county, often used by research people to determine sales potential.

Coefficient of Correlation—A figure used to measure the relationship between sales and variables that influence sales. Perfect correlation is indicated by the value 1.00, and 0. indicates complete absence of any relationship between the variables. Represented in formulas as R. (10e)

Coefficient of Determination—A figure used to measure the degree of relationship between sales and other variables, such as an economic indicator. Represented in formulas as R^2. (10e)

Coefficient of Statistic—A measure used to test the statistical significance of the relationship between sales and another variable, such as an economic indicator. Having derived the statistic by a complex formula, the *t-Distribution Table* is consulted to see if the variable is within the confidence limit desired. (See *The Management of Sales Forecasting*, by Eby and O'Neill, pages 120–121, 151–155.)

Confidence, limit of—The period during which sales can be expected to remain as predicted on the basis of probability.

Constant Process (or Model)—A forecasting time series that reveals no significant trend or cyclical changes, so a simple moving average could be used as the forecasting technique.

Correlation—The relationship between sales and the variables that affect sales, usually expressed in mathematical terms. (10d)

Correlation Analysis—Often used with regression analysis to measure the degree of the relationship between dependent and explanatory variables without assuming a cause-and-effect relationship. (10d)

Curve fitting—Use of the "least squares" method to develop a trend curve on a graph, for sales statistics.

Curvilinear regression—When past sales, averaged and plotted on a graph, show a curved trend line.

Cycles—The wavelike fluctuations of business or the economy over periods of time. (4d)

Cycle length—The span from peak to peak or bottom to bottom of a cycle.

Cyclical variation—That part of the changing pattern of sales that is attributable to a change in the business or economic cycle.

Decision tree—In long-range planning, a visualization of alternate decisions or possible events, usually designated as high-impact, medium-impact, and low-impact. The spokes radiating from each decision or event roughly resemble the branches of a tree.

Decomposition—A process used to break down the pattern of previous sales so the forecaster can determine what portion of sales for a given period reflects an overall increase or decrease in demand and what portion simply represents a seasonal fluctuation.

Degree of freedom—In testing for the validity of economic indicators to use in a time series, the number of time periods in the series minus the number of variables in the series. Every time another independent variable is added in a multiple regression model, another degree of freedom is lost. With a very large number of sales observations, the loss of degree of freedom is immaterial. (10f)

Demand Schedule—The differing amounts of an item that can be sold at changing price levels.

Dependent variable—A variable (usually sales), whose values are predicted on the basis of another variable or variables, such as economic statistics.

Differencing—Computing and tabulating the successive differences of a variable.

Diffusion index—A summary of the percentage of economic indicators that are rising or falling in a given time period.

Discounted least squares—A mathematical process for determining the average relationship between two or more variables, discounting the errors away from the current time period so that older observations receive proportionally less weight.

Dummy variable—An arbitrary figure added to a forecast to offset unusual and unpredictable events having a significant impact on sales, such as strikes, severe weather, price or wage freezes, etc. (10h)

Durbin-Watson Statistic—A statistical tool that is the sum of the squared first differences between an actual sales observation and its calculated value, divided by the sum of the differences (or residuals). (10h)

Econometrics—The process of finding and measuring the reliability of specific groups of economic statistics that have a bearing on sales. (10)

Economic indicator—A series of economic statistics or forecasts, such as Gross National Product or Housing Starts, that may parallel your past sales to a certain measurable extent and that could be used in projecting future sales. (10b)

Elasticity of demand—The degree by which change in price affects change in sales volume. If sales volume remains stable in spite of a price rise, the product is said to have elasticity of demand.

Endogenous variable—A variable that is dependent on another (or other) variable(s) in a sales forecasting equation.

End-Use Analysis—A forecasting method that projects demand by estimating the anticipated needs of end users of a product, such as a component used in the manufacture of other items. (7)

Exogenous variable—A variable that is independent of any other variable in a sales forecasting equation.

Explanatory variable—A group of economic statistics used to explain the variations of sales in the past.

Exponential smoothing—A weighted moving average of past sales, using a smoothing constant to modify the average in proportion to the error obtained in forecasting the previous periods sales, thus making it possible to give more weight to the more recent values. (9e)

Extrapolation—In sales forecasting, predicting sales on the assumption that what happened in the past will continue unchanged in the future.

Feedback—A situation where sales projections are considered goals or guides for action—the "self-fulfilling prophecy" syndrome. (3g)

Filter technique—A process to eliminate recurring differences between projected and actual sales results. Using an objective current forecasting equation, the forecaster goes backward in time to see how well it worked in past periods, notes those where the deviation has been excessive, and attempts to find the reason for the discrepancies. This is quantified and incorporated into the forecasting model.

FORAN Forecasting System—A comprehensive, computer-based method of breaking down a time series into trend-cycle, seasonal, and irregular elements and providing several alternative forecasts, along with testing procedures to help in choosing the right one. (9c)

Frequency distribution curve—A graphic representation of a brand's sales at various levels. On one axis of the graph is possible sales volume; on the other the probability of a given forecast level being reached (expressed as from 0. to 1.0, or 0% to 100%). The resulting bell-shaped curve shows the forecaster's confidence regarding the brand's sales prospects. The highest point of the curve represents the most likely sales level the forecaster thinks can be achieved. (12f)

Game theory—A method of arriving at rational marketing decisions in the face of uncertainty about competitive moves, by simulating the operations of key competitors and coming up with strategies to meet or counteract their possible actions.

Gompertz Curve—Based on the assumption that, once several weekly or monthly observations become available, a logarithmic model can be developed capable of extrapolating the entire growth curve, revealing both the slope of the curve and the point at which the maturity stage begins (leveling off of demand). In contrast with the Gompertz Curve, time-series models are not designed to forecast the entire growth curve.

Growth curve—A mathematical curve, as plotted on a graph, showing the average rate of sales growth of a product, company, or industry.

Independent variable—In forecasting sales, a set of statistics that is independent of your sales figures but which seems to have an influence on those figures.

Index number—A number used to indicate the relative change in sales or any other series as compared to its base-period value. Base value is usually designated as 100.

Input-Output Analysis—A method of projecting sales by using tables provided by the Department of Commerce that are designed to show what effect changes in demand in any of 86 major industries are likely to have on the sales of every other industry. (10c)

Inverse correlation—see *Negative correlation*.

Irregular variation—A fluctuation in the time series that can't be explained by trend, cyclical, or seasonal influences. There are random variations and nonrandom variations (see definitions). (4d and 8a)

Jury of Executive Opinion—A group of key company executives who combine their views to get a sounder forecast than one made by a single estimator. [Term coined by The Conference Board.] (5)

Lead-Lag indicators—In econometric forecasting, the finding of one or more economic indicators that tend to assume a familiar pattern to the data being forecast, but which increase or decrease ahead of it. For instance, a rise in housing starts could be expected to lead a rise in lumber sales. (10b, 10d)

Lead time—The interval between decision to buy and delivery of the goods, used in forecasting cumulative demand.

Least-squares method—A mathematical method of fitting a trend or economic indicator to past sales data, whereby the sum of all the squared differences between the sales data and the estimated trend are kept at a minimum. This tends to produce a more or less straight trend line when plotted on a graph. A shortcut method would be to divide the data in half, calculate the average of each half, and draw the trend line between these two average points on the graph.

Life-cycle—The phases most products and some industries go through, consisting of growth period, stabilization period, and decline period. (4f)

Life-cycle approach—The forecasting approach that takes into account the life-cycle of a product, adjusting estimates on the basis of its position in the life-cycle. (4f)

Linear programming—A technique of determining how to use limited resources to achieve a given objective, when such resources have alternate uses. Systematizes the process of picking the best course of action from all available courses.

Linear regression—Calculating the mean or average values of a variable over equal periods of time. When plotted on a graph, this approximates a straight line.

Logarithm (log)—A mathematical device (raising a fixed number by a certain power to produce a given number) that reduces computations by giving the rate of change rather than the absolute change.

Log paper—Graph paper in which the vertical lines or horizontal lines (axes) are spaced to adjust for logarithmic values. *Log-log paper* has both axes spaced for logarithmic values.

Market segmentation—Breakdown of markets according to the characteristics of buyers—economic, demographic, social, racial, etc.

Mean Absolute Deviation (MAD)—The error factor in exponential smoothing. It is the sum of the absolute differences between forecasted sales and actual sales, divided by the number of sales observations. Used instead of standard error calculations to save time and paperwork. (9j)

Model building—In sales forecasting, the development of rules or equations which express the relationships of certain variable and nonvariable factors in the marketing system and use them to predict their effect on sales.

Monte Carlo simulation—A repetitive, computerized simulation technique in which the effect on the forecast of one variable or another is calculated in terms of probability. (12f)

Moving average—A simple technique used to smooth out fluctuations in a time series. For instance, in doing a moving average of figures represented as ABCDEFG, the sum of ABC divided by 3 could be the first moving average, the sum of BCD divided by 3 the second, the sum of CDE divided by 3 the third, and so on. Of course, larger segments than 3 can be used; the larger the segment the better the smoothing effect. (8c)

Multiple correlation—Introduction of two or more sales-influencing variables into the forecasting model in order to improve the sales-projecting relationship.

Naive model—An early forecasting method that assumes that the figures for the forecast period will be the same as those of the preceding period. Also referred to as NF1, or Naive Forecast 1. NF2 is the naive forecast adjusted for seasonal fluctuations. Economists use naive forecasts as benchmarks for testing the accuracy of other forecasting methods. (9c)

Negative correlation—A relationship between two series of data where, when the values in one series increase, the values in the other decrease. Also called *Inverse correlation*.

Nonrandom irregular variations—Irregular movements in the data series that can't be explained by trend, cycle, or seasonal influences. Non-random irregularities are associated with a known cause, such as an unusually large order in one month or the results of an intensive sales contest. See also *Random irregular variations*. (4d)

Objective methods—Statistical or mathematical methods of forecasting, as opposed to subjective methods, which tend to be intuitive, based on the application of experience, intelligence, and judgment. A combination of both in forecasting is considered advantageous.

Paired index—A comparison of the behaviors of two economic indicators that might pace each other—the Coinciding Indicator and the Leading Indicator—to forecast the coincider turning point. Usually graphed, with index values used for simplicity, clustering around a base of 100 (see Eby and O'Neill, *Sales Forecasting,* page 51).

Panel approach—Members of various related industries are brought together by a trade paper, trade association, or outside research organization to discuss their needs for the coming year. Firms selling to these industries can then estimate the amount of sales they might get from them.

Parsimonious model—A forecasting model that adequately describes the time series but contains as few parameters as possible, such as variables or historical time periods.

Probability—In a sample of the market or other entity, determination of the possible margin of error in relation to the whole market or entity.

"Prudent Manager" forecasting—A small panel of specialists in the company assume the roles of members of the purchasing group in a customer or prospect company, prudently assessing ability to meet the customer's needs and sales objections and estimating the amount they might buy.

Random irregular variations—Irregular fluctuations in a sales curve that can't otherwise be explained as cyclical, trend, seasonal, or nonrandom irregular. These variations, which can't be associated with a known cause, are usually of short duration and relatively small impact. (4d)

Ratio graph—A logarithmic graph set up so that equal percentage changes show up as equal distances on the chart. See also *Log paper*.

Ratio to moving average—A tedious and rather costly method of computing seasonal adjustments, wherein the ratio of the actual value for a given month to a twelve-month moving average gives the forecaster a percentage indication of how the given month compares to data with the seasonal influence eliminated.

Regression analysis—Going back in a time series to analyze the relationship between sales and an explanatory variable (or economic indicator). Correlation analysis, often used with this technique, measures the degree of the relationship between such variables without assuming a cause-and-effect relationship. (10d).

Regression line—On a graph, the line or curve that shows the relationship between two variables, such as sales and an economic indicator. (10e).

Residual—The difference between the forecast calculation and the actual results. When graphed, residuals are shown distributed around a horizontal line that has an assigned value of 0, indicating no residual.

Saturation table—A forecasting tool for estimating sales to new customers. The table shows the number of people who have already bought the product compared to the number that might buy it, with an estimate of the number of first-time buyers in any given year. For instance, the trend to the two-car family lowered the saturation rate in the auto industry in recent years.

Scatter diagram—A chart to measure the relationship of two variables. One variable, such as sales, is measured on one axis of the chart and the other variable on the other axis. Where the two values intersect for each time period is indicated by a dot. If a reasonably straight line can be drawn between the dots, the variables can be considered in reasonably close relationship. (10d)

Secular trend—The long-term movement in sales or other variable, as contrasted with seasonal or cyclical occurrences. (4d)

Significance level—In correlation analysis, a measure of the probability that a seemingly close relationship between the variables is due to chance. The less probability of chance, the higher the significance level. *The t-Statistic* is used to measure this level. (10f)

Simulation—A computer-based method of testing the consequences of alternate business decisions, in contrast to field testing.

Slope of line—In graphing trends or correlations between variables, the degree of slant of the line showing a change in sales as influenced by time or another sales-influencing variable.

Smoothing—Ironing out the ups and downs in a time series by using moving averages, smoothing constants, etc. (9d)

Spectral analysis—An adjunct to other methods of time series analysis to determine the length and strength of cyclical patterns (see Jenkins and Watts, *Spectral Analysis and its Applications.* San Francisco: Holden-Day, 1968).

Standard deviation—A measurement of the fluctuations of a time series around its arithmetic average.

State-Space forecasting—Similar to the Box-Jenkins Model, but easier and faster to apply. A best forecast model is selected automatically by an "information criterion statistic." A de-trending procedure based on differencing is incorporated in the analysis (see Aoki, M., *Optimal Control and System Theory in Dynamic Economic Analysis.* New York: American Elsevier Publishing Co., 1976).

Step regression—A method of computerized testing of independent variables to determine their relationship to actual sales, plus the interrelationship between the independent variables. The process starts by picking the variable that seems most correlated to actual sales, building a forecast equation based on this simple relationship, then adding into the equation any other variables that seem to add significantly to the forecast. Computed at each step are change in sales per unit change in the independent variable, probable degree of error, element of chance involved (significance level), and percentage of variation in the forecast figure that is explained by inclusion of a variable.

Stochastic process—Selecting from a group of theoretically possible alternatives those elements or factors whose combination will most closely approximate the desired result (Stochastic means conjectural).

Subjective methods—In sales forecasting, the reliance on experience or hunches rather than statistical or mathematical methods of forecasting. See also *Objective methods.*

Tied indicator—A product or product line whose sales appear to be related to sales of the product being forecasted, such as the home appliance market and fractional horsepower motors.

Time series—A set of related statistics (such as sales, GNP, or population) listed by specific time periods [daily, weekly, monthly, quarterly, annually, etc.] (8a)

Top-down approach—This is where the forecast is based primarily on an estimate of business, industry, or economic conditions, with sales force and customer reports receiving secondary consideration. Regarded as better than bottom-up approach for long-range forecasting.

Tracking signal test—A test done in each period to determine the accuracy of the forecasting method being used. It is computed by dividing the expected forecast error by a measure of the variability of forecast error, such as the mean absolute deviation of forecast error. If the tracking error signal thus obtained deviates from zero by more than a prescribed amount, the forecaster considers modifications of the forecast model to improve accuracy.

Trend analysis—A simple method of sales forecasting in which past sales over a period of time are plotted (usually by moving averages) to show a trend line or curve which is then extended (extrapolated) into the future to indicate expected sales.

t-Statistic—See *Coefficient of statistic*. (10f)

Variable—Any ''ordered'' set of statistics, such as sales or a sales-influencing series, that has changed or may be expected to change its values over time.

Z Table—Otherwise known as Table of Areas Under a Normal Curve. This table, reproduced and explained in Eby and O'Neill, *The Management of Sales Forecasting* (pages 115–120) is used to determine the relationship between the standard error and the normal curve in calculating the frequency distribution curve (see definition above).

16

Additional Reading on
Sales Forecasting

Since 1960, the number of books and business publication articles on sales forecasting has grown apace. This has coincided with the increasing availability of computer services to make the complex and repetitive calculations required by many of the new mathematical techniques. For that reason, literature published before 1960 is apt to be a bit outdated.

Much of it is not easy reading for the average sales executive. It is aimed largely at the scholar or the statistician. Some knowledge of the basic principles and terminology of forecasting, as we've tried to impart in this study, is important to comprehension of some of the more scholarly treatises.

As the novice to sales forecasting delves further into the literature, he/she is apt to develop a fascination for this new art-science. Being able to predict the future has intrigued mankind for countless generations—and that, really, is what sales forecasting is all about.

16a Books

Sales Forecasting by D. L. Hurwood, E. S. Grossman, and E. L. Bailey. The Conference Board, 845 Third Ave., New York, NY 10022 ($45 for non-Associates of Conference Board, $15 for Associates), 1978. An excellent review of forecasting techniques, with many case histories. No index.

The Management of Sales Forecasting by F. H. Eby Jr. and W. J. O'Neill. Lexington, MA: D. C. Heath & Co., 1977. Sales forecasting according to product life cycle. Excellent step-by-step explanations of forecasting formulas. No index.

Forecasting and Time Series Analysis by D. C. Montgomery and L. A. Johnson. New York: McGraw-Hill Book Co., 1976. The forecasting technician's handbook, loaded with complex equations and exercises.

Marketing and Sales Forecasting: a Total Approach by Gordon J. Bolt. New York: Halsted Press Division of John Wiley & Sons, 1972. The marketing approach to sales forecasting. Very erudite and British. (Updated in *Marketing and Sales Forecasting Manual*, Prentice-Hall, 1982. See listing below.)

Practical Techniques of Sales Forecasting by R. S. Reichard. New York: McGraw-Hill Book Co., 1966. Good book for the novice. Easier to read than most books on the subject.

Practical Sales Forecasting by William Copulsky. New York: American Management Association, 1970. A brief overview of forecasting.

Short Term Forecasting by R. L. McLaughlin and J. J. Boyle. New York: American Marketing Association, 1968. Introducing the FORAN forecasting method.

Forecasting Methods for Management by S. C. Wheelwright and S. Makridakis. New York: John Wiley & Sons, 1973.

Time Series Analysis Forecasting and Control by G. E. P. Box and G. M. Jenkins. San Francisco: Holden-Day, Inc., 1976.

How to Make Early Warning Forecasts, Manual published by Cahners Publishing Co., 221 Columbus Ave., Boston, MA 02116.

Information Systems for Sales and Marketing Management by S. J. Pokempner. New York: The Conference Board, 1973.

Elements of Input-Output Analysis by W. H. Mierynk. New York: Random House, 1976.

Input-Output Analysis—a Non-Technical Description by M. S. Elliott-

Jones. New York: The Conference Board, 1971.

Evaluating New Product Proposals by E. P. McGuire. Report No. 604. New York: The Conference Board, 1973.

Marketing and Sales Forecasting by Frederick Keay (1972). Pergamon Press, Maxwell House, Fairview Park, Elmsford, NY 10523.

Methods of Correlation and Regression Analysis by M. Ezekiel and K. A. Fox. New York: John Wiley & Sons, Inc., 1959. A classic of its kind. Text and math easy to understand. Fourth edition is best.

Econometric Methods by J. Johnston. New York: McGraw-Hill, 1972. A forecaster's standard text. Latter half quite technical.

Preface to Econometrics by Michael J. Brennan. Cincinnati: South-Western Publishing Co., 1967. A good introduction to the subject.

Econometrics, 2nd ed., by R. J. Wonnacott and T. H. Wonnacott. New York: John Wiley & Sons, Inc., 1979. Well written, with plenty of illustrations. Good explanation of dummy variables.

An Introduction to Econometrics by Lawrence R. Klein. Englewood Cliffs, NJ: Prentice-Hall, Inc., 1962. Highly esteemed by economists. Klein helped to develop the Wharton Models.

New Product Forecasting: Models and Applications, edited by Yoram Wind, Vijay Mahajan, and Richard N. Cardozo. Lexington, MA: Lexington Books, 1981.

Marketing and Sales Forecasting Manual by Gordon J. Bolt. Englewood Cliffs, NJ: Prentice-Hall, Inc., 1982. Updated version of *Marketing and Sales Forecasting: A Total Approach,* listed above.

Early Warning Forecast, published by Cahners Economics, Cahners Publishing Co., P.O. Box 716, Back Bay Annex, Boston, MA 02117. Thirteenth Edition, 1983. How to construct your own business forecasts simply and accurately using the rate-of-change method (see Section 8g).

Out-of-Print Books

If a book you want is out of print and not in the library, you may be able to get a photocopy from University Microfilms International, Ann Arbor, Michigan. Phone them at 313–761–4700 for availability and price.

Course Manual

Sales Forecasting Manual by Robert L. McLaughlin is used in his seminars on Forecasting Techniques for Decision Makers, sponsored by Control

Data Corporation. It's ideal for either the novice or the seasoned forecaster, describing nearly every term and technique in layman's lingo, with 325 tables, charts, forms, and exhibits in 420 looseleaf pages. (Some of the illustrations in this book were taken from it.) If you want a copy, write to Robert L. McLaughlin, Box H, Cheshire, CT 06410 (203–272–3198) for information on availability and price.

A Few Sales Forecasting Courses

"Forecasting Techniques for Decision Making," a three-day seminar held in various key cities, sponsored by Control Data Management Institute, 6003 Executive Blvd., Rockville, MD 20852. Conducted by Robert L. McLaughlin (see Section 9b). For availability and cost, phone 1–800–638-6590.

"Early Warning Forecast Seminar," an intensive one- or two-day workshop where you learn forecasting step-by-step using data from your own company. Offered by Cahners Economics Division of Cahners Publishing Co., 221 Columbus Avenue, Boston, MA 02116. For availability and other details, phone James Haughey, Director of Economics, at 617–536–7780.

16b Articles

(published up to August 1983)

"Objective Forecasting: Problems and Solutions" by R. A. Lomas and D. Bell. *Industrial Management*, November 1978.

"Sales Forecasting Difficulties in a Developing Country" by J. J. Brasch. *Industrial Marketing Management*, October 1978.

"Some Human Problems in Industrial Sales Forecasting" by C. Gross and R. T. Peterson. *Industrial Marketing Management*, December 1978.

"Sales Forecasting—the Art and the Science" by E. Roseman. *Product Marketing*, June 1978.

"Development and Implementation of a Simple Short-Range Forecasting Model—a Case Study" by C. Kallina. *Interfaces*, May 1978.

"Effectiveness of Sales Forecasting Methods" by J. T. Rothe. *Industrial Marketing Management*, April 1978.

"How to Reduce Uncertainty in Sales Forecasting" by C. L. Hubbard and N. C. Mohn. *Management Review*, American Management Association, June 1978.

"Tracker: an Early Test Market Forecasting and Diagnostic Model for New Product Planning" by R. Blattberg and J. Golanty. *Journal of Marketing Research*, May 1978.

"Sales Forecasting Errors for New Product Projects" by B. Little and R. A. More, *Industrial Marketing Management*, February 1978.

"Sales Forecasting for the Smaller Organization" by R. A. Lomas and G. A. Lancaster. *Industrial Management*, February 1978.

"Sales Planning Factors for Selected Manufacturing and Industrial Groups" (with table). *Sales and Marketing Management Magazine*, April 24, 1978.

"Appraising the Sales Forecast" by R. S. Savesky. *Managerial Planning*, November 1977.

"Projecting Consumptions of Competing Products" by H. Hinomoto. *Long Range Planning*, Pergamon Press, October 1977.

"Sales Forecasting Practices of Large U.S. Industrial Firms" by J. Pan. *Financial Management*, Fall 1977.

"Evaluation of Effectiveness of a Model-Based Salesmen's Planning System by Field Experimentation" (United Airlines). *Interfaces*, November 1977.

"New Product Planning Decisions Under Uncertainty" by R. G. Hudson and others. *Interfaces*, November 1977.

"Forecasting New Product Sales Prior to Test Market" by E. M. Tauber, *Food Product Development* (P.O. Box 555, Arlington Heights, IL 60005), April 1977.

"Incorporating Judgment in Sales Forecasts—Application of the Delphi Method at American Hoist & Derrick." *Interfaces*, May 1977.

"Input-Output Modeling—New Forecasting Tool" by N. C. Mohn and others. *University of Michigan Business Review*, July 1976.

"On-Target Sales Forecasting—Basis for Better Planning" by K. T. Stephens and R. W. Wilde. *Product Marketing*, March 1977.

"Sales Forecasts" by K. J. Rosier. *Accountant Magazine*, December 9, 1976.

"The Jantzen Method of Short Range Forecasting" by Carl Vreeland. *Journal of Marketing*, April 1963.

"Forecasting Sales by Exponentially Weighted Moving Averages" by P. R. Winters. *Management Science*, Vol. 6, No. 3, 1960.

"Adaptive Filtering—an Integrated Autoregressive/Moving Average Filter for Time-Series Filtering" by S. C. Wheelwright and S. Makridakis, *Operational Research Quarterly*, 1977.

"A Simultaneous Regression Study of Advertising and Sales of Cigarettes" by F. M. Bass. *Journal of Marketing Research*, August 1969.

"Use of Input-Output Concepts in Sales Forecasting" by E. C. Ranard. *Journal of Marketing Research*, February 1972.

"The Effects of Sampling Variations on Sales Forecasts for New Consumer Products" by R. Shoemaker and R. Staelin, *Journal of Marketing Research*, May 1976.

"The Use of Consumer Panels for Brand-Share Predictions" by J. H. Parfitt and B. J. K. Collins, *Journal of Marketing Research*, May 1968.

"How to Choose the Right Forecasting Technique" by J. C. Chambers, S. K. Mullick, and D. D. Smith. *Harvard Business Review*, Vol. 65, No. 4, 1971: 531–37.

"The Efficient Use of an Imperfect Forecast" by H. E. Thompson and W. Beranek. *Management Science*, Vol. 13, No. 3, 1966.

"Forecasting Derived Product Demand in Commercial Construction," by R. D. Rosenberg. *Industrial Management*, February 1982.

"Competitors, Customers and Markdowns" by W. V. Westerfield. *Chain Store Age*, December 1981.

"Distributors Get Pointers on How to Set up Sales, Financial Forecasts, Long-Range Plans" by J. O. Sweet. *Air Conditioning, Heating & Refrigeration*, January 25, 1982.

"Using Bonuses to Inspire Sharper Sales Forecasts is a Risky Assignment" by J. K. Moynahan. *Sales and Marketing Management*, December 7, 1981.

"Crystal Ball vs. System—The Forecasting Dilemma" by G. Frisbie and V. A. Mabert. *Business Horizons*, September–October 1981.

"Developing a Sales Forecasting System" by R. F. Reilly. *Management Plan*, July–August 1981.

"Reducing Overaction in Contract Markets" by S. H. McIntyre. *Industrial Marketing Management*, October 1981.

"Adaptive Sales Forecasting with Many Stock-Outs" by P. C. Bell. *Operations Research*, Journal of the Operations Research Society of America, October 1981.

"Short-Term Forecasting and Stock Control in the Real World" by G. Burton and T. Allil. *Accountancy* (Great Britain), June 1981.

"Adapting Forecasting Methods to the Small Firm" by J. G. Wacker and J. S. Cromartie. *Business Management*, July 1979.

"Backcasting: a Sales Performance Evaluation Tool at Coca-Cola" by C. L. Hubbard et al. *Interfaces*, August 1979.

"Bottom-Up Sales Forecasting Through Scenario Analysis" by C. A. De Kluyver. *Industrial Marketing Management*, April 1980.

"Comparison of Opinion and Regression Forecasting for an Industrial Product" by J. R. Walton. *Industrial Marketing Management*, November 1979.

"See Aro Hit the Sales Target" by S. Scanlon. *Sales and Marketing Management*, August 20, 1979.

"Use of Cycle Analysis (Moving Average)" by P. H. Jedel. *Business Economics*, March 1980.

"Your Sales Forecast-Marketing Budget Relationship: Is it Consistent?" by J. S. Lowe and others. *Management Accounting*, January 1980.

"Aggregation and Proration in Forecasting" by E. Schlifer and R. W. Wolff. *Management Science*, June 1979.

"Application of Discriminant Analysis to the Prediction of Sales Forecast Uncertainty in New Product Situations" by R. A. More and B. Little. *Operations Research*, January 1980.

"Issues in Sales Territory Modeling and Forecasting Using Box-Jenkins Analysis" by M. Moriarty and A. Adams. *Journal of Market Research*, May 1979.

"Evaluating a New Market: a Forecast System for Non-Impact Computer Printers" by S. S. Oren and others. *Interfaces*, December 1980.

"Forecasts will enable Distributors to Sharpen Inventory Sales Plans" by T. A. Mahoney. *Air Conditioning, Heating & Refrigeration*, October 20, 1980.

"Market Forecasting—Needs Determine Method" by O. R. Welsh. *Plastics World*, March 1981.

"Start With a System" by T. D. Roebuck. *Sales and Marketing Management*. February 2, 1981.

"How to Set Volume-Sensitive ROI Targets" by R. J. Lambrix and S. S. Singhri. *Harvard Business Review*, March–April 1981.

"Modeling and Forecasting Sales Data by Time-Series Analysis" by S. G. Kapoor and others. *Journal of Market Research*, February 1981.

"Relative Information Contributions of Consumer Purchase Intentions and Management Judgment as Explanators of Sales" by M. A. Sewall. *Journal of Market Research*, May 1981.

"Projection of U.S. Metropolitan Markets to 1986" (population, buying income, and retail sales). *Sales and Marketing Management*, October 25, 1982.

"How to Discover What Your Sales People are Planning (and Doing)" by J. D. Alampi. *Sales and Marketing Management*, December 7, 1981.

"Timeshare Feasibility Study: Forecasting Sales Performance" by C. W. Hart. *Cornell Hotel and Restaurant Administration Quarterly* (Cornell

University School of Hotel Administration, Ithaca, NY 14853), May 1982.

"Twelve Prescriptions for Better-Forecast-Strategy-Goal Link" *Marketing News*, March 18, 1983.

"Implementation Exchange: the Implementation Profile" (a computerized sales forecasting model) by R. L. Schultz and D. P. Slevin. *Interfaces*, February 1983.

"Forecasting Sales on the Basis of Advertising Budgets: the Case of Crest Toothpaste" by M. M. Schreiber. *Business Economics*, May 1982.

"Forecasting With Diagonal Multiple Time Series Models, an Extension of Univariate Models" by S. Umashankar and J. Ledolter. *Journal of Marketing Research*, February 1983.

"Probing the Past for the Future" (Emerson Electric) by R. F. Soergel. *Sales and Marketing Management*, March 14, 1983.

"Non-Computer Forecasting Approaches to Use Right Now" by J. M. Jenks, *Business Marketing*, August 1983.

"Computer-aided Sales Forecasting: How the Skeptics can Learn to Love it" by S. Buchin and T. A. Davidson. *Business Marketing*, August 1983.

"Pre-test Market Models: Validation and Managerial Implications" by G. L. Urban and G. M. Katz. *Journal of Marketing Research*, August 1983.

Titles of articles on sales forecasting that appeared after this list was published may be found in the *Business Periodicals Index* in most public libraries.

16c Where to Find Articles

If any of the articles listed in this bibliography are of interest to you, you can find back issues of the publications in most large libraries. Where they aren't available, get in touch with the publication, specifying issue date and title of the article. Here are their addresses:

Accounting Review, American Accounting Association, 5717 Bessie Drive, Sarasota, FL 33583.

Air Conditioning, Heating and Refrigeration News, P.O. Box 2600, 755 West Big Beaver Road, Troy, MI 48084.

Business Economics, National Association of Business Economists, 28349 Chagrin Blvd., Suite 201, Cleveland, OH 44122.

Business Horizons, School of Business, Indiana University, Bloomington, IN 47405.

Chain Store Age Executive, 425 Park Ave., New York, NY 10022.

Financial Management, College of Business Administration, University of South Florida, 4202 Fowler Ave., Tampa, FL 33620.

Harvard Business Review P.O. Box 3000, Woburn, MA 01888.

Industrial Management & Data Systems, MCB Publications Ltd., 198/200 Keighley Road, Bradford, W. Yorkshire BD9 4JQ ENGLAND.

Industrial Marketing Management, Elsevier North-Holland, Inc., 52 Vanderbilt Ave., New York, NY 10017.

Interfaces, Institute of Management Sciences, 146 Westminster St., Providence, RI 02903.

Journal of Marketing Research, American Marketing Association, 250 South Wacker Drive, Chicago, IL 60606.

Long Range Planning, Pergamon Press, Headington Hill Hall, Oxford OX3 OBW ENGLAND.

Management Accounting, National Association of Accountants, 919 Third Ave., New York, NY 10022.

Management Review, American Management Association, 135 West 50th St., New York, NY 10020.

Management Science, Institute of Management Sciences, 146 Westminster St., Providence, RI 02903.

Management Planning, Planning Executive Institute, P. O. Box 70, Oxford, OH 45056.

Operations Research, Journal of Operations Research Society of America, 428 East Preston St., Baltimore, MD 21202.

Plastics World, Box 5391, Denver, CO 80217.

Product Marketing, Charleston Publishing Co., 124 East 40th St., New York, NY 10016.

Sales and Marketing Management, 633 Third Ave., New York, NY 10017.

Index